D0540706

TWAYNE'S WORLD AUTHORS SERIES

A Survey of the World's Literature

SPAIN

Mateo Alemán

(TWAS 48)

TWAYNE'S WORLD AUTHORS SERIES (TWAS)

The purpose of TWAS is to survey the major writers —novelists, dramatists, historians, poets, philosophers, and critics—of the nations of the world. Among the national literatures covered are those of Australia, Canada, China, Eastern Europe, France, Germany, Greece, India, Italy, Japan, Latin America, New Zealand, Poland, Russia, Scandinavia, Spain, and the African nations, as well as Hebrew, Yiddish, and Latin Classical literatures. This survey is complemented by Twayne's United States Authors Series and English Authors Series.

The intent of each volume in these series is to present a critical-analytical study of the works of the writer; to include biographical and historical material that may be necessary for understanding, appreciation, and critical appraisal of the writer; and to present all material in clear, concise English—but not to vitiate the scholarly content of the work by doing so.

Mateo Alemán

By DONALD McGRADY
University of California, Santa Barbara

Twayne Publishers, Inc. :: New York

Library of Congress Catalog Number: 67-25196

MANUFACTURED IN THE UNITED STATES OF AMERICA

Preface

In recent years Mateo Alemán has been restored to his proper place as one of the two greatest novelists of Spain's Golden Age. Many important studies on *Guzmán de Alfarache* attest to a renewed interest in the novel that stands second only to *Don Quixote* in Spanish literature prior to the nineteenth century. In the present book I attempt to summarize previous studies on *Guzmán* and its creator at the same time that I introduce new points of view.

One of my principal aims is to show that the relationship between Mateo Alemán's life and that of his picaresque protagonist is much more intimate than has been suspected. The complexity of Guzmán's tortured soul is surely a reflection of Alemán's own, particularly in Part II of the novel. Another important thesis here set forth is that Part I of *Guzmán* was written more with the purpose of entertaining the reader than of preaching to him—a point that has been all too forgotten by critics of the twentieth century. Part II of *Guzmán* doubtless would have followed this same pattern had it not been for Juan Martí's apocryphal continuation of the novel. However, the spurious *Guzmán* caused Alemán to revise his plans. The result was a continuation in large part couched in allegorical terms and devoted to avenging the literary theft. To be artistic, an allegory must be meaningful on the literal plane as well as on the metaphorical. Alemán fulfills this requirement so successfully that most of the action in Part II has not been appreciated on any other level than that of the picaresque adventures. Alemán uses his position as creator of the world of Guzmán to impose penalties as though he were God. Within the universe of his novel Alemán reigns supreme, and he punishes those who have offended him. Part II of *Guzmán* is a dreamworld in which the frustrated author takes revenge on his enemies by making them characters, thus bringing them under his jurisdiction. A considerable portion of the continuation is therefore a *roman à clef.* In spite of the greater complexity of the continuation, it is my contention that Part I of *Guzmán* is the more skillfully written.

For reasons of coherence and convenience, it has seemed advisable to divide my study into three parts: a biography of Alemán (Chapter 1), general considerations on *Guzmán de Alfarache,* including an analysis of the picaro's psychology (Chapters 2-3), and a detailed commentary on the action of *Guzmán* (Chapters 4-7). Since this book is directed to a large audience, I have not hesitated to state for the benefit of the novice what may seem obvious to the specialist. I mention Alemán's minor works, which are nonliterary in nature, only when they throw light on his life.

Although it is inevitable that some of the charm of the Spanish original should be lost in translation, it is hoped that the quotes from James Mabbe's lively seventeenth century rendition will retain a flavor approximate to Alemán's. In some cases it has been necessary to correct Mabbe's inaccuracies; these rectifications appear in square brackets. Other translations in the text are mine, unless otherwise specified. Portions of Chapter 7 have appeared in somewhat different form in *Comparative Literature* and *Romance Notes.* I am deeply grateful to Editor Gerald E. Wade for his invaluable suggestions for the improvement of the book.

Donald McGrady

Santa Barbara, California
March 1967

Chronology

1547	September 28, Mateo Alemán is baptized in Seville.
1557	His father, Hernando Alemán, becomes physician to the Royal Prison in Seville.
1564	Mateo is graduated from the University of Maese Rodrigo in Seville. Starts medical studies at the same University.
1565	Probably studies medicine at the University of Salamanca.
1566	Continues studies at the University of Alcalá de Henares.
1567	Must leave studies temporarily because of his father's illness and death.
1568	Finishes his medical courses, but does not graduate. Begins a business career. Receives two loans, payable within a year. He will be released from one debt if he marries Catalina de Espinosa.
1571	Still has not paid the liability and faces the alternatives of marrying Miss Espinosa or going to prison. He marries.
1574	Elected head of a religious fraternity.
1573–1579	More business ventures.
1580	Enrolls in the University of Maese Rodrigo to study law, but does not complete the year. Imprisoned for debts in October; still in jail on December 29.
1582	Unsuccessful attempt to emigrate to Mexico.
1583	Receives a judgeship in the region of Extremadura; subsequently he is imprisoned for overstepping his powers.
1584	Obtains an accountantship with the government. Moves to Madrid and continues trading to supplement his salary.
1586	Buys a lot and builds a house in Madrid.
1590	Birth of his daughter Ana Urbana.
1591	Journeys to Cartagena; he narrowly escapes death when struck by a burning cannon plug.

1592 His mother dies. He travels to Seville.
1593 He is named a judge to investigate the working conditions of slaves at the royal quicksilver mines in Almadén.
1597 Finishes Part I of *Guzmán de Alfarache*.
1598 Writes a prologue for the *Proverbios morales* (*Moral Proverbs*) of Alonso de Barros.
1599 Publication of *Guzmán de Alfarache*, which becomes a best seller almost overnight. Birth of his son Antonio.
1601 Catches the printers of a pirated edition of *Guzmán* and makes a settlement with them. Moves to Seville, fleeing from his creditors in Madrid.
1602 Becomes intimate with Francisca Calderón. His cousin Juan Bautista del Rosso lends him money. An apocryphal continuation of *Guzmán* appears. Alemán is imprisoned for debts, and his wife refuses to post bail.
1603 Juan Bautista del Rosso pays Alemán's debt and secures his release from prison.
1604 Publication of *San Antonio de Padua* (*Saint Anthony of Padua*). Alemán goes to Portugal to promote the sale of this book. His daughter Margarita is born. He publishes Part II of *Guzmán* in Lisbon, and stays in this city over a year.
1605–1606 Unsuccessful business transactions.
1607 By bribing a government official, Alemán obtains permission to emigrate with his family to New Spain. The voyage is canceled because of menacing Dutch pirates.
1608 Emigrates to Mexico. Receives the protection of Archbishop García Guerra.
1609 Publication of his *Ortografía castellana* (*Castilian Orthography*) and a prologue for Luis de Belmonte Bermúdez' *Vida del Padre Maestro Ignacio de Loyola* (*Life of Father Ignatius of Loyola*).
1613 Publication of *Sucesos de D. Frai García Gera* (*Happenings of Fray García Guerra*).
1615 Alemán is a resident of the village of Chalco, Mexico. His date of death is unknown.

To Marina

Contents

Preface 7

Chronology 9

1. Alemán's Life 13
2. General Considerations on *Guzmán de Alfarache* 44
3. The Psychology of Guzmán 88
4. Part I of *Guzmán de Alfarache* 100
5. Part II of *Guzmán*: Response to the Apocryphal Continuation 113
6. Part II of *Guzmán*: Conclusion 130
7. The Interpolated Novelettes in *Guzmán* 145

Notes and References 169

Selected Bibliography 183

Index 187

CHAPTER 1

Alemán's Life

I *Birth and Family*

MATEO Alemán was baptized on September 28, 1547, in the church of San Salvador, in Seville.[1] His date of birth is not recorded; however, babies were usually christened within a couple of weeks after birth. He was the third child of Dr. Hernando Alemán and his second wife, Juana de Enero (also written Henero or Nero).

Dr. Hernando Alemán, a native Sevillian, had practiced medicine in the 1530's in the small village of Jerez, in the region of Extremadura. Since his practice there was not successful, he returned to Seville around 1540. His first wife, Beatriz de León, died about the same time, leaving him a small daughter named Jerónima. Five of Dr. Alemán's brothers and sisters were living in Seville: Alonso, a merchant; Juan, a physician; García Jerónimo, a priest; and Leonor and Beatriz, spinsters, who lived with their brother Alonso. Dr. Alemán did not prosper in his home town; as late as 1556 one of his maids had to sue him for her salary. Things finally began to look up toward the end of 1557, when he was appointed physician to the Royal Prison in Seville.

The Alemán family was known to be of Jewish origin. This is of great importance, for in 1492 the Jews in Spain had been forced to accept the Christian religion or leave the country. Those who remained were placed under rigorous surveillance to insure that their acceptance of Christianity was sincere, and that they did not secretly practice the Judaic faith. The Spanish Inquisition was charged with the task of supervising the purity of the Spanish Jews' conversion to Christianity, and meted out punishments to offenders. The maximum penalty for infringement of orthodoxy was burning at the stake. Even the smallest trace of Hebrew blood brought disgrace on a Spaniard, and those known to have this taint were not eligible for noble titles. Indications are that the paternal branch of Mateo Alemán's family descended from a certain Alemán known as *Poca Sangre* ("Little Blood"), who was burned by the Inquisition in Seville toward the end of the fifteenth century. The Alemanes tried to disavow this infamous ancestry by inventing a fake genealogical tree, according to which the family descended from German soldiers who served with the Emperor Charles I in his campaigns in northern Europe. The slight bit of factual basis for this fantasy is that *alemán* means "German" in Spanish.

As might be expected, the New Christians, or Christianized Jews and their descendants, tended to marry within their own group. It is therefore not surprising to learn that Dr. Alemán's second wife, Juana de Enero, was also of Jewish origin. Her family was originally from Florence, but like many other Italian families engaged in commerce, they had emigrated to Spain after the expulsion of the Jews had greatly diminished the mercantile class there. The Italian upper classes had no prejudice against trading—in marked contrast to the Spanish nobility—and so Florentine and Genoese merchants took the place of the expelled Jews in Spain. Juana de Enero's father, Juan López de Enero, was a businessman in Seville.

In addition to Mateo, Dr. Alemán and his wife Juana had three children: Leonor, Violante, and Juan Agustín. It is noteworthy that the couple always included clergymen among the sponsors of their children's baptism. Existing baptismal certificates show that Violante had one sponsor from the clergy, Mateo had four, and Juan Agustín, two. This partiality for ecclesiastical sponsors was doubtless due in part to Dr. Alemán's wide acquaintance with the clergy through his brother García Jerónimo, who was a priest. But at the same time, it appears to be an attempt by the Alemán family to give proof of their orthodoxy.

II *Mateo's Education*

The only facts known about Mateo Alemán's elementary education are the reminiscences he inserted in his treatise *Ortografía castellana* (*Castilian Orthography*), published in Mexico in 1609. There he recalls that his teachers demanded that he learn many different styles of handwriting, a procedure he considered a waste of time. After learning to read and write, Mateo followed the usual course of study: a thorough grounding in Latin grammar and literature. A friend of Alemán tells that he grew up in the study of the classics,[2] and the many references in his works to Greek and Latin writers bear out this statement. It has been suggested that Alemán studied classics in the academy of Juan de Mal Lara, the famous Latin scholar and paroemiologist, but this is purely conjectural. In any case, Alemán received his Bachelor's degree in Arts and Philosophy from the University of Maese Rodrigo in Seville in June of 1564.

The future writer decided to study medicine, possibly at his father's behest. After completing his first year at the University of Maese Rodrigo, he probably studied for a year at Salamanca, Spain's oldest and most renowned university (it had been founded in 1230). The following year (1566-1567) Alemán studied at the University of Alcalá de Henares. Judging from autobiographical descriptions in *Guzmán de Alfarache* (II, iii, 4),[3] Alemán must have taken an active part in student diversions, stealing pies and melons, hazing freshmen, and keeping prohibited weapons under the bed. However, alarming news came to interrupt his pleasant college life: in February of 1567 he was called home because of his father's illness, and in March Dr. Alemán died. He left a meager inheritance, which was divided among his widow and children. In spite of the straitened circumstances caused by his father's death, Alemán returned to the University to finish his third year of medical studies, and the following year he completed the courses for the M.D. degree. Having arrived at this point in his studies, Alemán suddenly decided, for unknown reasons, not to pursue a medical career. It is possible that he had studied medicine only to please his father. In *Guzmán* Alemán expresses antipathy toward the medical profession,[4] but this might be interpreted as the result of a sour grapes attitude. And it is pertinent to recall that satire against doctors had been commonplace in European literature since the Middle Ages.

III *Business Career and Marriage*

Shortly after his twenty-first birthday, Alemán embarked on a business career. In October, 1568, he contracted two large debts; presumably they provided the capital for his subsequent buying and selling operations. Both debts were to be paid within a year. One of the loan contracts is of particular interest, for it stipulated that Alemán was to marry, within a year's time, a certain Catalina de Espinosa. Biographers have concluded from this clause that Alemán had become involved with Miss Espinosa, the illegitimate child of a wealthy Sevillian, but refused to marry her. Miss Espinosa's guardian, Captain Alonso Hernández de Ayala, devised this clever method of entrapping the reluctant gallant: he made Alemán a loan from Miss Espinosa's estate, reasoning that he would waste the money and be unable to repay it at the end of the year. The guardian would then confront him with the alternatives of going to jail for the unpaid debt or marrying Miss Espinosa and paying the debt from her dowry. The plan worked to perfection in that Alemán did not pay the loan; but neither did he marry Miss Espinosa within the stipulated time. Captain Hernández de Ayala waited almost two years more, and then filed a suit against Alemán in June of 1571. Caught between the sword and the wall, the averse beau at last made good his promise and assumed the yoke of matrimony. Such a marriage was naturally doomed to failure. It appears that Alemán did not live long with his wife, although they maintained a business relationship for something more than thirty years. The novelist's attitude toward his wife is reflected in the disillusioned view he takes of matrimony in *Guzmán.*

After his marriage Alemán engaged in many types of commercial activities. In 1573 he sold a female Moorish slave for thirty-two ducats. In 1576 he agreed to collect duties on wool for six years. Two years later he set up bylaws for a religious fraternity (he had been elected head of this organization in 1574); the next year he bought a chapel for this same fraternity.[5]

IV *Debtor's Prison*

The diversity of his undertakings seems to be indicative of

Alemán's lack of success. Perhaps for this reason he decided in January of 1580 to return to the University of Maese Rodrigo, with the intention of studying law. One biographer has suggested that his purpose was to learn, not how to apply the law, but how to circumvent it in his wheelings and dealings.[6] In any case, this determination was short-lived; Alemán dropped out of school before the year was up, probably because of economic pressures. His creditors caught up with him in October of 1580 and had him thrown into the Royal Prison of Seville, the same establishment where his father had worked years before. As was customary, the jailers shackled Alemán. In *Guzmán de Alfarache* he explains the reason for this seemingly unnecessary measure: in order to have the fetters removed, an inmate had to pay a handsome tip. Furthermore, bond was to be posted. Catalina had her husband's shackles removed by pledging all her present and future property. But two months later Alemán was again in irons, without having left the prison, possibly because of new claims against him. At this point his uncle Alonso came to the rescue, putting up enough bond to have his fetters removed again. It is no compliment to Alemán that his relatives—several of whom resided in Seville—did not provide bond for him until two months after his imprisonment.

V *The Attempt to Emigrate*

For the period from 1571, the date of his forced marriage, to 1581, when he was released from debtors' prison, Mateo Alemán was down on his luck. It appears that during this entire time his center of activity was Seville. After his release from jail, it was natural that he should want to change his horizons and get a fresh start in life. For a Spaniard of the sixteenth and seventeenth centuries, the obvious way to do this was to move to the New World, the land of opportunity. Every day in Seville, the seat of administration of Spain's vast colonial empire, Alemán had the chance to talk to men who a few years before had departed for Mexico or Peru and were now back in Spain, comfortably well off. He had a cousin, Dr. Alonso Alemán, who had gone to Mexico in 1571 and had done very well for himself in the Royal and Pontifical University of Mexico. Perhaps this cousin could help him obtain a government job. So in March of 1582 Alemán requested permission to emigrate to Mexico. In order to receive a license to go to New Spain, it was necessary to prove that he had no Jewish blood. He presented two neighbors who swore to this, but the authorities were not convinced and denied him permission.[7]

Alemán's application to emigrate discloses some details about his physical appearance. It states that he was tall, had a long nose, a dark red beard, and a small scar on the left thumb. A portrait he included in several of his works reveals that he had widely separated and melancholy eyes, a high forehead, a wide and sensual mouth, ears that stuck out slightly, and a typically Semitic nose. He wore a moustache and a goatee.

VI *The First Judgeship*

There is a Spanish proverb that says that no bad luck lasts a hundred years. Alemán's fortunes finally took a turn for the better in the spring of 1583, when he was made a judge. The position was only temporary, but it carried a great deal of prestige and could easily have been the stepping-stone to a permanent position. Alemán's commissions took him to the towns of Llerena and Usagre, in Extremadura. His duties entailed the audit of a deceased royal employee's account and the recovery from his heirs of some funds still owed to the government. From the first moment Alemán was overbearing and excessively severe. He overstepped his powers, levying fines and court costs in matters that had nothing to do with his functions. The offended parties appealed directly to King Philip II, who called the arbitrary judge to account for his misconduct. As if this were not enough, Alemán went even further in a subsequent adventure. Seemingly without good reason, and certainly without any authority, he released several prisoners from the Royal Prison of Usagre. When the constable and commander of the province protested against this action, he mistreated them in word and deed and threw them into chains, in place of the freed prisoners. This flagrant act of injustice did not go unpunished: in October of 1583 Alemán was arrested in Mérida, by order of the King, and then transferred to Madrid. In November he was still in prison, but later was released on bail. The case did not conclude until June of 1584.[8]

The motives of Alemán's deplorable conduct can only be conjectured. Perhaps he saw corruption in these small provincial towns and decided to root it out, dispensing with the normal channels of justice. It has also been suggested that his conduct was an expression of resentment as a member of the abused class of New Christians.[9] Whatever the reason, his behavior can not be justified morally or legally. In Alemán's conduct can be detected the arrogance of the well-educated man who looks down on those of humble culture and station.

VII *The Accountantship*

In view of Alemán's lamentable record as a judge, it is surprising to discover that even before the conclusion of his trial for abuse of office he was named to another government position: that of accountant. It is likely that he took up his new duties in early 1584. Since Philip II's administration was centered in Madrid, Alemán moved to the capital city. In October of 1586 he bought a lot and started construction of a house on it. Apparently his wife Catalina did not move to Madrid with him, but stayed in Seville, where she had some property.

Alemán's occupation occasionally took him to other parts of Spain. A particularly important trip, because of its consequences, was that of January, 1591, to the port city of Cartagena. Alemán had been invited, along with several municipal authorities, to visit a Flemish ship lying in the harbor. When they were returning to land, the ship fired a salvo in salute and Alemán was struck in the head by a burning cannon plug. Although he could easily have been killed on the spot, he escaped unhurt. Alemán attributed his salvation to Saint Anthony of Padua, whose intervention he had invoked in the moment of danger. He made a vow to write a biography of the saint, as an expression of gratitude for his deliverance. Alemán did not fulfill this oath until more than a decade later, but the fact that he spontaneously called on the saint in a perilous situation and later made and fulfilled the vow is evidence of his deep and sincere Catholicism.

In April of 1592 Alemán traveled to Seville on business. His mother had died in that city some time before. During this period Alemán continued his private trading operations to supplement his government salary. From 1589 to 1599 he acted as a commission agent to buy houses, rented and sublet houses and pasture lands, and took on the guardianship of a minor. It appears that he also made usurious loans disguised as the sale of household goods. In spite of his sharp practices, Alemán was not financially successful. It is perhaps surprising that his profound religiousness did not interfere with his immoral business tactics. The same duality is found in Alemán's creature, Guzmán, and is the fundamental artistic basis of his novel.[10]

VIII *The Second Judgeship*

In January of 1593 Alemán was appointed to another *ad hoc* judgeship similar to the one he carried out so discreditably ten years earlier. His duties entailed the investigation of working conditions at the royal quicksilver mines in Almadén. Since the middle of the century the German Fuggers had worked these mines for the kings of Spain. In 1566 they had received thirty galley slaves from the Crown to help exploit the mineral; this number was raised to forty in 1583. The slaves were to fulfill their sentences by toiling in the mines instead of rowing on galleys. Their working conditions were to be humane, though rigorous. There had been so many complaints against the noncompliance with these minimum standards that in 1591 a government department resolved to send a judge to Almadén to make an inquiry. With their powerful influences, the Fuggers delayed the investigation for two years, and in the interim they introduced reforms to bring the slaves' working conditions up to the stipulated norms. Thus when the future novelist arrived on the scene in early February of 1593, he found only the memory of past abuses. Alemán carried out his charge diligently and lawfully. The administrators tried to hide important documents concerning the slaves, but Alemán put them under house arrest and sought out the papers. There is no indication that he exceeded his powers, as in 1583. Apparently his investigation, which ended in March, 1593, came to nought, as there is no record of measures being taken against the Augsburg bankers for their past inhumanities. It has been suggested that there may be some relationship between Alemán's interrogations of the galley slaves in Almadén and his novel.[11]

IX *Literary Activities*

During this same period of commercial activity, Alemán began to show increased signs of literary interests. He had been a voracious reader since childhood, but only in middle age did his vast readings start to bear fruit. Perhaps his residence in Madrid, the literary center of Spain, prompted his dormant muse. His first published efforts were modest indeed: a translation of two odes by Horace, printed without date or place, and a prologue for the *Proverbios morales* (*Moral Proverbs*) of his friend Alonso de Barros, printed in 1598. These minor works give no indication of the genius of their author, but do foreshadow two themes that he would develop fully in his novel. Both of the odes he selected for translation treat of the vanities of earthly possessions, while in the prologue to Barro's *Proverbios* Alemán states that self-interest is the prime mover of mankind.

The publication of Part I of *Guzmán de Alfarache* in March of 1599 catapulted Mateo Alemán from obscurity into the dazzling light of the literary world. The novel had been carefully written, and was the distillation of many years of reading and meditation. Like *Don Quixote,* it is the product of a middle-aged man's ripened reflections on life. *Guzmán* was doubtless in preparation for several years. Alemán's extensive use of literary and historical allusion means that he must have spent considerable time just assimilating his source material

Alemán's book was finished in late 1597,[12] but it did not appear in print until well over a year later. This delay was not out of the ordinary, for a book had to overcome many obstacles in order to be published in Spain during the sixteenth and seventeenth centuries.[13] In 1558 Philip II had decreed that nothing could be printed in Spain without the permission of his Royal Council. This meant that a book had to have regal and ecclesiastical approval. A manuscript was first presented to the Royal Council, who named a censor, usually a member of the clergy. This reader examined the book to make sure there was nothing in it contrary to the teachings of the Church or detrimental to the interests of the State. After his approval, the King's Royal Council granted permission for publication. In addition, ecclesiastical approval was required in some dioceses. The book was printed without title page or preliminaries, and a copy was carefully collated with the original manuscript by a reader of the Royal Council. Only then were the title page and preliminaries printed. Included in the preliminaries were the ecclesiastical and royal licenses, the page of errata (made up by the Royal Council's reader), and the price, also set by the Council. The author, or the person to whom he sold the rights, received from the King the exclusive privilege to publish the book within a determined length of time, usually around ten years. Printers of pirated editions were subject to confiscation of the books and printing forms, plus a large fine. The denouncer of a piracy received one third of the fine. In practice, however, these penalties were rarely levied and pirated editions were often more numerous than legal ones. Authors therefore seldom derived great financial benefit from the sale of their works.

Guzmán de Alfarache received Fray Diego Dávila's approval on January 13, 1598, the license of the Royal Council on February 16 of the same year, and the latter's final approval on March 4, 1599. During this interval of over a year the King had died, so Alemán had to change the title page, where he called himself the servant of Philip II, to read Philip III. It is interesting that he requested the exclusive privilege of sale of *Guzmán* for twenty years, but received it for only six.[14]

No other Spanish classic has achieved such immediate popularity as *Guzmán de Alfarache*. The first edition was published in March of 1599; within two months, others, most of them pirated, began to appear. There were five editions in 1599, eleven the following year (including printings in Antwerp, Brussels, Coimbra, Lisbon, Paris, and an unidentified Italian city), and twenty-six by the time of publication of Part II of *Guzmán* in December of 1604.[15] According to Luis de Valdés, the author of a laudatory prologue to Part II, these twenty-six editions sold over 50,000 copies. Not even *Don Quixote* was to obtain such prompt acceptance. During Alemán's lifetime three translations were made of

Guzmán: into French (1600), Italian (1606), and German (1615).[16]

Unfortunately, only three of these editions were made with Alemán's consent,[17] and of course he did not receive royalties from the piracies. As so often happened with popular books before the advent of enforced copyright laws, only the booksellers reaped considerable profits from the sale of *Guzmán*, leaving its author almost as poor as before.

Although the book did not make him rich, it did bring Alemán enduring fame. *Guzmán de Alfarache* made its author's name famous not only in Spain, but also in Italy, France, Flanders, and Germany, where he received the epithet of "the divine Spaniard." In a public ceremony in the University of Salamanca, an Augustinian priest declared that no nonreligious book of greater usefulness and entertainment had ever been published. In that same University, Alemán's style was so highly praised that it was claimed that he had done for the Spanish language what Demosthenes had done for the Greek and Cicero for the Latin.[18] In 1648, Baltasar Gracián, one of the most cultured Spaniards of his time, affirmed that Alemán's style was so superb that it combined "Greek inventiveness, Italian eloquence, French erudition, and Spanish wit."[19] To no other classic writer does Gracián attribute these four prime literary qualities. Gracián went so far as to prefer the picaresque novelist over Cervantes. Even today Alemán's prose is considered to be one of the purest and most refined in the language.

Alemán's fame was not confined to Europe, but extended even to the far-off New World. In spite of the prohibition against the importation of works of fiction in the Spanish colonies, many books of this type arrived on every ship. From 1600 on, *Guzmán de Alfarache* was shipped to the Indies in large quantities. The appearance of *Don Quixote* in 1605 did not diminish the popularity of the picaresque novel; indeed, *Guzmán* enjoyed even better sales among colonial readers than *Don Quixote*. It is a commonplace that Cervantes' immortal novel administered the *coup de grâce* to the fantastic books of chivalry, both in Spain and in her colonies. However, it now appears that even before the publication of *Don Quixote, Guzmán* had largely succeeded in exiling from the Spanish colonies this formerly popular type of romance.[20]

X *Lovers and Offspring*

While his novel was amusing readers throughout Europe and the New World, Alemán continued in economic throes. In February of 1601 his circumstances were so bad that he resorted to a debtor's last recourse: the fake sale. This rather common fraud was designed to cover up a usurious loan under the semblance of a bill of sale. Alemán "bought" some gold silk worth 102,204 *maravedís* from a certain López named Diego or Miguel (both names appear in documents relating to the transaction);[21] in reality he received a loan for much less, due at the end of five months. Three months after the deal with López, Alemán also owed a substantial sum for the rental of several houses. Toward the end of 1601 the novelist returned to Seville, where he set up a household separate from his wife's and hired an elderly housekeeper, Gregoria Volante. One of his primary reasons for leaving Madrid was to get away from his creditors, particularly López.

What was the cause of the writer's penury? Besides his accountantship, which paid him a modest salary, Alemán received income from his labors as a real estate and commission agent; his novel also produced some earnings. It would seem that Alemán indulged in some expensive vice. The most common weakness among Golden Age writers was women: Cervantes, Lope de Vega, Alarcón, Quevedo, Calderón, all sired illegitimate offspring. Alemán was typical in this respect, having three natural children: Ana Urbana, born around 1590; Antonio, in 1599; and Margarita, in 1604.[22]

No information is available about Alemán's first mistresses, the mothers of Ana Urbana and Antonio. The birth dates of these children indicate that they were born while Alemán was living in Madrid. More is known about his last paramour, Francisca Calderón. According to a description of 1607,[23] she was of olive complexion and had a small birthmark under her left ear. The novelist may have met her some time in 1602, when she was twenty-five and he fifty-five. Alemán knew Miss Calderón at least fairly well in November, because in that month he assisted her in a lawsuit over a young female slave. Their relations progressed rapidly, for a month later she gave him power of attorney to manage her small estate. This power of attorney lasted ten months, while Francisca's brother, a priest, was absent from Seville. Later documents show that Francisca lived with Alemán, and that her sister María also made her residence with them. Francisca was probably the mother of the novelist's youngest child, Margarita, born in Seville in 1604.[24]

XI *Juan Bautista del Rosso*

It was customary in Alemán's day for writers to dedicate their works to a powerful patron. If the recipient of the dedication was so inclined, he would take the writer under his protection and help provide for his needs. Mateo Alemán, like Cervantes, was unfortunate in his choices of protectors for his different works, for there is no evidence that he received support from this quarter. However, the picaresque novelist was more favored by luck than was Cervantes, for upon his return to Seville he found an invaluable friend in a cousin named Juan Bautista del Rosso. This cousin came from a wealthy family of Florentine origin and was a very successful businessman in his own right. Although Rosso was not the generous patron that some biographers have taken him to be, he did give the novelist a helping hand when all others had deserted him.

The first notice of Alemán's connections with Rosso is a document of August, 1602, in which the author granted his cousin the right to print an edition of Part I of *Guzmán.* Although it is not so stated, Rosso had probably already done his cousin some pecuniary favor, in order to receive such a handsome recompense. In September, Rosso lent Alemán 400 ducats, payable at the end of October.[25] The fact that he recorded the loan shows that Rosso was not a liberal Maecenas, as some have thought, but a practical businessman.

XII *The Apocryphal* Guzmán

Up to this point, the year 1602 had been a favorable one for Alemán: he had managed to elude his Madrilenian creditors, to meet a new paramour, and to find someone willing to lend him money in spite of his being a bad risk. However, this prosperity in his various endeavors was only temporary; two severe reverses awaited him. Alemán's first setback was a literary one: in late August there appeared in Valencia an apocryphal continuation of *Guzmán de Alfarache*. The author hid his true identity under the pseudonym of "Mateo Luján de Sayavedra," an obvious imitation of Alemán's name. In the authentic Part II of his novel Alemán indicates that the spurious author was Juan Martí, a native of Valencia. Scholars have uncovered an obscure Valencian lawyer of this name, about whose life very little is known. Alemán declares that Martí plagiarized his completed manuscript for Part II, and that he consequently had to rewrite his authentic continuation, in order to make it different from the fraudulent work. It seems more likely, however, that Martí knew only the general outline of part of Alemán's book, which was probably still incomplete at the time Martí commenced his writing. There are no documents to indicate how Martí came into possession of Alemán's ideas. Perhaps the novelist read from the manuscript to his friends, or lent it to them to read. In the authentic Part II Alemán seems to insinuate that Martí did him a good turn to gain his friendship and then treacherously used this favored position to steal his plans for the continuation (see Chapter 5, Sections IV-VI below).

Juan Martí's purpose was partly literary and partly commercial. As a work of art, the apocryphal *Guzmán* shows some talent, but falls far short of Alemán's novel. As concerns its sales, Martí's *Guzmán* was a surprising success, due principally, no doubt, to the fact that readers took it to be the authentic continuation. There were four editions of the false *Guzmán* in 1602 and ten in 1603; but there was only one in 1604, the year in which the true continuation appeared. Martí did not profit greatly from the remarkable sales of his book. Poetic justice was served: the majority of the editions appear to have been pirated.[26] Martí died in December of 1604, about the time that Alemán's Part II was being printed.

XIII *Debtor's Prison*

The second stroke of misfortune that Alemán suffered in 1602 was his imprisonment; this occurred toward the middle of December. The writer had not paid the López fake-sale loan of February, 1601, and so his bondsman, Pedro de Baeza, had been obliged to pay it. Baeza then asked for a judgment against Alemán. This order had been issued in June of 1602, but did not arrive in Seville until six months later. So Alemán had been living the second half of the year on borrowed time, as well as money. The novelist appealed to his wife Catalina to bail him out of prison, but she would have no part of him. Therefore in January, 1603, Alemán revoked the power of attorney he had given Catalina to collect rent from a house he owned. Lacking further resources, he had to resign himself to prison life. He whiled away the hours working on a new book, entitled *San Antonio de Padua* (*St. Anthony of Padua*). It will be remembered that Alemán had vowed in 1591 to compose the Saint's biography; as usual, the writer was late in fulfilling his promise.

On January 25 of 1603, after Alemán had been in prison for over a month, Juan Bautista del Rosso finally agreed to take over his debt, though he retained the power to sue the novelist for the money owed. It is interesting that Rosso paid the debt with 500 copies of *Guzmán.* Rosso refused to pay the judiciary costs involved in finding Alemán and executing the writ against him, so the writer had to prevail on the executor, Francisco Demar, to accept payments for these costs in three yearly installments. Rosso's delay in coming to Alemán's rescue was probably due to his doubts about the picaresque novelist's ability to pay him back.[27]

XIV *The Significance of a Pirated Edition of* Guzmán

It has already been noted that Mateo Alemán derived little profit from the sale of his famous picaresque novel, because the great majority of the editions were pirated. Nevertheless, a recently discovered bill of sale[28] discloses that Alemán did obtain compensation for at least one pirated edition. Moreover, this document may furnish the key to several seemingly unrelated events in the novelist's life. Briefly stated, the facts are as follows: Two Madrilenian booksellers, Miguel Martínez and Francisco López, were so foolish as to print an unauthorized edition of *Guzmán* under Alemán's very nose, when he was living in Madrid in 1601. Although they published the edition under false names, the novelist caught the pirates and turned a good profit from their illegitimate labors. He threatened to denounce them to the authorities, but Martínez and López persuaded him to accept a settlement instead. The entire transaction was concealed under the guise of a bill of sale, drawn up before a notary, in which Alemán figured as selling copies of the piracy to the unauthorized printers. The arrangement they worked out was advantageous to both parties: Alemán received 106,500 *maravedís* —two thirds of the value of the books—and the publishers kept fifteen hundred copies of their piracy. Had Alemán denounced Martínez and López, he would only have been entitled to a third of the fine of fifty thousand *maravedís* imposed by law on the printers of unauthorized editions. Martínez and López, on the other hand, would have lost their entire printing, plus the fine. The government of Philip III would have been the principal beneficiary of the denunciation.

Up to this point, the bill of sale is clear in its implications, in spite of the efforts of the booksellers—both well-known pirates— to disguise the true nature of the operation. However, other clauses in the notarial instrument have veiled meanings that are much more difficult to decipher. One curious provision states that Alemán could not sell in Spain an edition of the same octavo size for two years, unless Martínez and López had sold out their copies; however, after one year, the novelist could export such an edition to the Indies. If Alemán violated this clause, Martínez and López had the right to print an edition of fifteen hundred copies. It would appear that this stipulation was unnecessary— unless Alemán had in his possession copies of the Martínez-López piracy. The inference that suggests itself is that the author did have copies of the piracy, and that Martínez and López wanted to sell their supply first. Since the contract specifically declares that no money changed hands before the notary, it is conceivable that Alemán accepted copies of the piracy as payment. If many volumes of this edition were to appear later on in the writer's biography, this conjecture would seem to be well founded.

As a matter of fact, a large number of copies of *Guzmán* do turn up later in the novelist's life—it will be remembered that Alemán was freed from debtor's prison in January of 1603 by the payment of five hundred volumes of *Guzmán.* Unfortunately, the available data do not fall into a clear pattern. These books were valued at 210 *maravedís* apiece; but no known edition of *Guzmán* had this price (the cost of a book was always specified in its preliminaries). Therefore it is impossible to determine to which edition the books in question belonged. There are two possibilities: the edition printed by Juan Bautista del Rosso in 1602, whose selling price was ninety-nine *maravedís,* and the Martínez-López piracy, evaluated at 105 *maravedís*—just half the price of the copies that liberated Alemán from jail. Is it possible that these books were of the cheap Martínez-López edition in octavo, and that the wily book dealers evaluated them at twice their value when they delivered them to Alemán? This would be in accord with the other known instances of their unethical conduct. Assuming that the novelist received books in lieu of cash from Martínez and López, and that he could not sell these books to the public for two years, then the copies of *Guzmán* used to pay the López debt in 1603 could well have been those received from the book pirates in 1601. The fact that Rosso was the one who paid Alemán's debt does not invalidate this hypothesis; the writer could have sold or pledged the books to his cousin.

Exploring further the possible connections between the different events in the novelist's life, it seems reasonable to postulate a relation between the Martínez-López piracy and the loan Alemán contracted in February of 1601. The loan was made by a Diego or Miguel López, in the amount of 102,204 *maravedís.* This López may have been a relative of Francisco López, the book pirate. Could the piracy have been provoked by an announcement by Alemán that he did not intend to repay the loan? Francisco López, who had experience in piracies, could have suggested this means for recovering the money Alemán refused to return. Perhaps Francisco López had a direct interest in the loan; otherwise, it is difficult to understand why such an experienced pirate would be so imprudent as to print an illegal edition when the author was nearby. Martínez and López must have started their piracy shortly after Alemán obtained the loan, since the book was finished in May (a volume of this length was usually done in a couple of months).

Assuming a relation between the loan and the piracy, the sequence of events would have been the following: (1) On February 3, 1601, Diego or Miguel López loaned 102,204 *maravedís* to Alemán, under the guise of a sale; the loan was payable within five months. (2) Shortly afterward, Alemán probably let it be known that he did not intend to repay the loan. (3) Francisco López and Miguel Martínez, who may have been friends or relatives of the lender, decided to print a pirated edition of *Guzmán*, possibly with the intent of recovering the amount of the loan; they probably started work in March. (4) In late May, Alemán discovered the piracy; López and Martínez made a settlement, possibly of five hundred copies of the piracy valued at 210 *maravedís* (twice their true worth), plus a small commission of fifteen hundred *maravedís* in cash. (5) In late 1601 the picaresque novelist moved to Seville without paying López; his bondsman made good the debt and started action to recover his money. (6) In mid-December of 1602, Alemán was imprisoned for the debt. (7) On January 25, 1603, Alemán's cousin Rosso paid the obligation with five hundred copies of *Guzmán*, possibly of the Martínez-López piracy.

It is tempting to look for other evidence of the enmity between Mateo Alemán and the pirate editors. There is conceivably a connection between the booksellers and the author of the apocryphal *Guzmán*. Martínez and López certainly had good motivation to desire such vengeance as could be had only by wounding the author in the most sensitive place: his novel. Juan Martí may have received the idea of a spurious continuation from the revenge-seeking pirate editors; it is likely that he began his apocryphal *Guzmán* some time in 1601—about the time of the antagonism between the pirate publishers and Alemán. As will be seen later, in the analysis of the authentic Part II, Alemán converts the history of the spurious *Guzmán* into an allegory, and it appears that there may be allusions to López and Martínez. The evidence is very tenuous and therefore can not be pushed too far; the present conjectures are set forth only as a possibility for further research. In any case, there does exist definite proof of the continued hostility between the picaresque novelist and the pirates: in September of 1603, Francisco López printed an edition of the apocryphal *Guzmán,* as if to flaunt it in Mateo Alemán's face.

XV *Publication of* San Antonio de Padua

On March 3, 1603, Juan Bautista del Rosso signed a contract with a Sevillian printer for the publication of Alemán's *San Antonio de Padua.* The printing press was to be set up in the writer's home. The printer agreed to start work on March 20, and to complete one signature (section of a book) daily. Rosso was in a hurry to get the work done; he specified that the printer could accept no other work until this book was finished, and penalties would be assessed against him if he did not produce the amount of work agreed upon. On the other hand, Rosso would have to pay the printer daily wages even if he could not provide material for him. This last clause seems to mean that Alemán had not yet completed the manuscript. Luis de Valdés corroborates this supposition in his prologue to Part II of *Guzmán*; Valdés discloses that, for the last part of the book, Alemán had to compose at night the material that was to go to the printer the next day. It is therefore evident that *San Antonio* was printed before it received ecclesiastical and governmental approval. These licenses were not given until November and December. In January of 1604, Alemán granted Rosso the right to print the book. But it appears that the work was finished long before then, except for the preliminary pages, which were always printed separately.

Why was Rosso in such a hurry for Alemán to conclude his book and have it published? The answer is obvious: he was anxious to recover some of his bad debts from the profligate author. There is no record of Alemán's returning the four hundred ducats Rosso had lent him in September, 1602, to be repaid a month later. Neither had he paid back the 105,000 *maravedís* (the value of the five hundred copies of *Guzmán*) that Rosso advanced to free him from debtor's prison in January of 1603.

These are the debts that appear in documents; there may have been more. It is quite probable that Rosso paid for Alemán's release from prison with the understanding that the latter would repay him with the profits from his new book; this seems to be the meaning of Rosso's agreement with the printer, made ten months before Alemán officially gave him permission to publish the book. And although the novelist does not state that he ceded his royalty rights to his cousin, later documents show that Rosso collected receipts from the book's sales (see Section XVII below).

XVI *Alemán and Lope de Vega*

Included among the preliminaries of *San Antonio de Padua* were the customary laudatory poems from the author's friends. The best poem by far was that of Lope de Vega, Spain's greatest dramatist. Alemán had probably become a friend of Lope during his long residence in Madrid. At the time of printing of the preliminaries of *San Antonio,* in early 1604, Lope was in Seville and composed a poem in honor of Alemán. The reason for Lope's extended visit in Seville was a beautiful actress by the name of Micaela de Luján.[29] Micaela soon gave the picaresque author the opportunity to return Lope's favor. The actress' husband had recently died in Peru, and Micaela wished to inherit his estate by becoming the legal guardian of their children. For this purpose she needed a bondsman: the most likely candidate was Lope, who happened to be the father of several of the children that Micaela attributed to her husband. Lope in turn needed a witness who could attest to his financial resources. He called on Alemán, possibly because of the latter's great powers of imagination. Alemán rose magnificently to the occasion, swearing with a straight face that the always needy dramatist was a wealthy man, and the possessor of houses in Madrid worth two thousand ducats.

Some scholars have speculated that Lope and Micaela lived with Alemán and Francisca while they were in Seville. This seems unlikely, in view of the large households that both writers had, but it is known for certain that they lived in the same neighborhood.[30]

XVII *The Trip to Portugal. Part II of* Guzmán

Saint Anthony of Padua was a native of Portugal and was particularly venerated in his homeland. Therefore Alemán dedicated his book to the Portuguese people and traveled to Lisbon, in hopes of promoting the sale of his book there. In April of 1604, Alemán put his affairs in order, giving power of attorney to Francisca Calderón to rent or sell his houses and all the rest of his possessions. He also gave her a document in which he pretended to have received a year's rent from her, which indicates that he expected to be gone about a twelvemonth. But it appears that he stayed in the Portuguese capital longer than he had planned.

The most important event of his sojourn there, and perhaps another motive for his trip, was the publication of Part II of *Guzmán,* which came off the presses in late December. The continuation of *Guzmán de Alfarache* bore the subtitle of *Atalaya de la vida humana* (*Watchtower on Human Life*), which emphasized its moral purpose. Ever since the appearance of the apocryphal continuation two years earlier, Alemán had been chafing at the bit to take revenge on the unscrupulous imitator, Juan Martí. As will be seen later, his vengeance was complete. Alemán rewrote his Part II sometime between the spring of 1603, when he probably finished *San Antonio,* and September, 1604, the date of approval of the continuation. There are many coincidences in the digressions of *San Antonio* and Part II of *Guzmán.*

During Alemán's visit to Portugal, Juan Bautista del Rosso was busy sending large shipments of *San Antonio* to the Indies. Some ship-manifests of April, 1605, disclose consignments of almost 400 copies to different parts of the New World. In the following July, Rosso started shipping the second part of *Guzmán* to the Spanish colonies; the first consignment of 490 copies is ample proof of the popularity of Alemán's picaresque novel in the Indies.[31] It also indicates that Rosso was probably the true owner of the first edition of *Guzmán,* Part II.

The last information regarding Alemán's relations with his cousin Rosso is a document dated March 2, 1607, in which

Rosso asked a Lisbon bookseller for the payment or return of thirty copies of *San Antonio* that Alemán had consigned to him in April of 1605. The subsequent lack of evidence of any relationship between them probably means that the practical businessman decided to have no more financial dealings with the impractical novelist.

XVIII *Unsuccessful Business Ventures*

It is not known when Alemán returned from Portugal; the first time he appears again in Seville is in October of 1605. In that month he bought a piece of land that was to give him nothing but headaches. Over a year later, on December 20, 1606, he declared in a notarial document that he had bought the land, not for himself, but for a certain Atanasio de Averoni. Only two days later Alemán annulled the sale because there was a mortgage on the land.

A document of August, 1606, tells of the conclusion of another unsuccessful business venture. In January of 1604, Alemán had received power of attorney to collect the salary supposedly due a certain pilot in the royal fleet. The following day he found out that a considerable part of the salary already belonged to someone else. He could not collect the money and so turned the matter over to Juan Bautista del Rosso before leaving for Portugal in April. Rosso was also unable to obtain payment. Therefore, after two and a half years of wasted effort and money, in August of 1606, Alemán gave up the contract to another person, undoubtedly because it was worth nothing. It is likely that Alemán had bought the pilot's salary at a considerable discount, and then, finding it uncollectible, tried to foist the worthless commercial paper off on his creditors.

There is no evidence of how Alemán fared in his other real estate and commission ventures after his return from Lisbon. He owned one or two houses in Seville and another in Madrid, and they would pay him some small amount of rent. It appears that he received little or no income from the first editions of *San Antonio* and the continuation of *Guzmán,* since he turned the receipts over to his cousin Rosso for payment of back debts. A second edition of *San Antonio* was printed with his permission in Seville in 1605, and may have given him royalties.

XIX *The Trip to Mexico*

All in all, Alemán's prospects were bleak indeed. His commercial enterprises had gone from bad to worse, his books yielded but small royalties, and he could no longer count on the help of his cousin Juan Bautista del Rosso. To make things worse, Alemán had accumulated a large household: his paramour Francisca, her sister María, two or three children, and a housekeeper. Looking for a solution to his problem, Alemán turned his thoughts to New Spain, just as he had done twenty-five years before, in 1582. Besides his poverty, the writer had other good reasons for considering a move to Mexico. A cousin, Dr. Alonso Alemán, was a professor of law and an administrator in the Royal and Pontifical University of Mexico (see Section V above). Dr. Alemán had married the granddaughter of a presumably rich conquistador and owned some mines. This distinguished individual was in an excellent position to help the impoverished novelist. It is possible that the writer's decision to go to Mexico in 1582 had been based on an offer of aid from this cousin.

So in 1607, Alemán again decided to leave for the New World. In his petition for a license to emigrate, made in April, he mentioned that a very wealthy cousin had invited him to come to Mexico. Although he did not state the name of his cousin, it is safe to assume that he was referring to Dr. Alonso Alemán. But the creator of *Guzmán* did not tell all he knew about his cousin, to wit, that Dr. Alemán had died around July of 1605, almost two years earlier. This could mean that the writer was counting on a legacy from his late cousin's estate,[32] or some other type of aid. It is unlikely that at age sixty he would have resolved to leave all in Spain and go to an unknown country, if he did not have assurance that a good livelihood awaited him there.

Before the novelist could reach the promised land, however, he had to overcome the ban against the emigration of New Christians. Fortunately for Alemán, there were ways of getting around even the most rigid prohibitions. For many years those of Jewish descent had migrated to America by the simple expedient of bribing individuals in key positions.[33] This is what Alemán did. Shortly before receiving permission to depart to the Indies, he made two large gifts to Pedro de Ledesma, the official who granted the authorization. On April 10, 1607, Alemán deeded his properties in Madrid to Ledesma, and on May 14 he transferred to him the rights of publication of *San Antonio* and Part II of *Guzmán*. In addition, on his application the novelist exchanged his second surname of Enero—a sure mark of Hebrew ancestry in Seville—for that of Ayala.[34] It is fortunate for Spanish literature that twenty-five years earlier Alemán had been bankrupt and not in a position to corrupt emigration officials. Given the handicaps of authorship that existed in the New World, it is unlikely that he would have composed his masterpiece there.

A lesser difficulty that the author faced was how to take Francisca Calderón along without arousing suspicion. She could not be passed off as his wife, because Catalina, his legal spouse, was still alive. Therefore Alemán reduced his paramour's age from thirty to twenty-four and labeled her his daughter, Francisca Alemán. Other members of his entourage were his illegitimate offspring Margarita and Antonio, a niece named Catalina, who was apparently the illegitimate daughter of his brother Juan Agustín, and two servants. It is not known why he did not take Ana Urbana, his oldest child.

The picaresque novelist had his defects, but they apparently did not include stinginess or ingratitude. The day before his scheduled departure, Alemán granted power of attorney to collect rent from his houses in Seville to Gregoria Volante, his housekeeper, to María Calderón, his paramour's sister, and to Domingo García, an unidentified member of his household, probably a servant. He also gave Miss Calderón the right to live in one of the houses rent free, or to rent it and enjoy its income.

It has been seen that bad luck plagued Mateo Alemán much of his life. And now just when he was on the point of obtaining a well-deserved rest after many years of adversity, misfortune struck again. All was in readiness for the departure of the 1607 fleet to New Spain when word arrived that the sailing had been canceled because of the menace of Dutch pirates on the Spanish coast. Alemán and his companions had to wait impatiently another twelve months. The writer probably spent the year at the small town of Trigueros, near the southwest corner of Spain, where he had relatives. He passed the time working on a new book, entitled *Ortografía castellana* (*Castilian Orthography*). Finally, in June of 1608, the long-awaited moment arrived, and Alemán and his oddly-assorted family embarked for the New World. In addition to Alemán, several other distinguished individuals were aboard the fleet. Returning to his native Mexico was Juan Ruiz de Alarcón, later to become a famous dramatist. Another important personage on the voyage was the new Archbishop of Mexico, Fray García Guerra. Alemán became well acquainted with the illustrious prelate, and this association doubtless was of great advantage to him later in Mexico, particularly after García Guerra's additional appointment as Viceroy of New Spain. The voyage to Mexico lasted the normal time—over two months. To while away part of the hours, Alemán probably continued work on his new book. He doubtless spent some of his enforced leisure perusing *Don Quixote,* a novel that was rapidly beginning to compete in popularity with his own *Guzmán de Alfarache.* His copy of Cervantes' masterpiece was confiscated on arrival in Mexico by an overzealous inspector from the Inquisition, obviously with the intent of impressing the Archbishop. The book was subsequently returned to Alemán at the request of the Archbishop himself.[35] Judging from the account he later gave in his *Sucesos de D. Frai García Gera* (*Happenings of Fray García Guerra*),[36] published in 1613, Alemán probably accompanied the church dignitary in his triumphal march from Vera Cruz to Mexico City. In this partial biography of the prelate, Alemán recalled with picturesque detail the many ceremonies and festivities that awaited the Archbishop in every hamlet and village.

XX *Last Years in Mexico*

There is a scarcity of documents about Alemán subsequent to his departure from Spain. However, the little available information indicates that things went well with the aging novelist in Mexico, probably due in part to the Archbishop's protection, and in part to assistance bequeathed by his deceased cousin.

In the preface of his *Ortografía castellana,* published in 1609, Alemán referred to himself as a "gay and lucky pilgrim" and talked about his "good fortune." This is the first time that he used such enthusiastic terms to describe his lot. At the age of sixty-two, Fortune had finally smiled on the picaresque writer. It is fitting that the days of one who toiled so much should have a happy ending. This does not mean that Alemán's happiness was complete: in another part of the same preface he alluded to the enemies who would not stop attacking him until his demise.

Also of 1609, is a brief foreword that Alemán penned for the *Vida del Padre Maestro Ignacio de Loyola* (*Life of Father Ignatius of Loyola*), a pious biography by his young friend Luis de Belmonte Bermúdez. In November of that same year, Alemán was working as an accountant in the University,[37] a post he probably received through the offices of his late cousin. In December, Alemán leased a house in Mexico City for a period of three years.[38] From his first deposit was to be deducted the cost of installing new doors and windows and rebuilding a wall that separated the yard from the adjoining property. An addendum to the original agreement, dated January 31, 1610, indicates that the repairs had not been made and Alemán himself was going to have them done, subtracting the expenses from his rental payments.

Alemán's last known work is his *Sucesos de D. Frai García Gera* (1613). In it he describes the Archbishop's arrival in Mexico, his appointment as Viceroy of New Spain, the fatal illness that followed shortly after he assumed office, and the elaborate funeral. It concludes with a eulogy which dwells on the vanity of earthly possessions. Alemán's final production thus returns to a theme that had been fundamental in his writings ever since his choice of odes to translate from Horace. His biography of the Archbishop-Viceroy is not so much the tribute of a friend as the homage of an indebted subject to a great benefactor. On the title page of the *Sucesos,* the picaresque novelist calls himself an accountant in the King's service, which means that he still held his position at the University. With the publication of this work, Alemán practically drops out of sight. The only remaining scrap of information is a report that in

1615 he was living in the small village of Chalco.[39] Thereafter the genial author of *Guzmán de Alfarache* disappears from view.

Traces remain of his daughter Margarita, who became a nun in the convent of Ste Theresa in Mexico City in 1626. Since this convent was one of the more aristocratic, requiring a dowry of four thousand pesos, it would seem that Alemán prospered in New Spain. Sister Margarita inherited her father's gift for writing, as seen in a biography she composed of the convent's founder. She was still living in 1658.[40]

XXI *Did Alemán Visit Italy?*

The great majority of Mateo Alemán's biographers and critics assume that he visited Italy. The basis for this supposition is an extensive description that Guzmán makes of the city of Florence in Part II of the novel. This widely-held conjecture not only bears directly on the novelist's biography, but also concerns an important question of literary interpretation: the validity of supposing that certain types of experiences undergone by fictional characters are necessarily reflections of the authors' experiences. It is therefore necessary to examine the possibility that Alemán went to Italy.

The proponents of the theory point out the detail with which the novelist describes the principal churches, convents, and monuments of Florence, and conclude that such minute description can come only from direct contact with these objects. However, the descriptions show indications of having been extracted from written sources; their most striking characteristic is that they consist largely of historical narrative and statistical detail, precisely the kind of information found in reference books.[41]

None of the theory's proponents has suggested a convincing date for Alemán's supposed trip. The *terminus a quo* for the visit is 1594, the year of elevation of a statue that appears in the description; the *terminus ad quem* is 1604, the date of publication of Part II of *Guzmán*. It happens that this is one of the best documented periods in Alemán's life. There are indications of his whereabouts for every year in this ten-year period except for 1596, when he was hard at work on his novel. It is extremely unlikely that, being so occupied with his writing, Alemán would have had time to take a protracted trip to Italy. Another cogent argument against the trip is that neither Alemán nor any of his contemporaries mentions such a visit. On the other hand, there is abundant documentary evidence concerning his proposed trip to the New World in 1582, his sojourn in Lisbon from 1604 to 1605, and his voyage to Mexico in 1608. No explanation has been advanced as to what the purpose of an Italian trip would have been.

The evidence leads to the conclusion that Mateo Alemán did not visit Italy. The supposition of such a trip did not even arise until nearly two and a half centuries after the writer's death. The sole basis of this conjecture is a description of Florence in *Guzmán,* a description that in itself argues against Alemán's direct knowledge of the city. If further proof were needed, the author himself furnishes it. During a moment of rare candidness in II, ii, 2, Alemán injects himself bodily into the fictional relation and declares that he is not familiar with countries other than Spain (see Chapter 2, Section XI below).

Once it has been established that Alemán did not go to Italy, there remains the problem of why he inserted the laudatory description of Florence in his novel. The praise of cities as a literary topic has a long tradition, dating from classical literature. It was extensively used by such Spanish Golden Age authors as Luis de León, Cervantes, Lope de Vega, Tirso, Alarcón, and Alcalá Yáñez.[42] What is a little unusual about Alemán's description is that he praises an Italian city, not a Spanish one. This is all the more striking because no important action of *Guzmán* takes place in Florence. An acquaintance with Alemán's life yields the explanation to the problem. The maternal branch of his family was of Florentine origin; the novelist's mother, Juana de Enero (or Nero), and her sister Agustina (mother of Juan Bautista del Rosso) were natives of Seville, but past generations of their family had emigrated from Italy. Several of Alemán's known friends and business associates were also of Florentine families. There appears to have been almost a clannishness among these Florentines and their descendants, perhaps attributable to their Jewish origin. The eulogistic description was thus a tribute to the native city of one branch of Alemán's family.

One descendant of Florentines who would be particularly pleased to see praises of the city was the writer's cousin, Juan Bautista del Rosso. Both sides of Rosso's family were from Florence; his father, Lorenzo, had migrated to Spain around 1540. The son's interest in Florence is reflected in his many business connections there. Alemán finished writing and revising Part II of *Guzmán* in 1604—precisely the end of the period in which he was receiving favors from his cousin Rosso (1602-1604). The novelist's gratitude to Rosso and his desire of further favors offer a good explanation for the description of Florence.

XXII *Alemán and Cervantes*

There is a curious parallelism in the lives of the greatest novelists of Spain's Golden Age: Mateo Alemán and Miguel de Cervantes. They were born within two weeks of each other, in September and October of 1547. The fathers of both writers were doctors of small means. Both novelists inherited this curse of poverty and found life a continuous struggle against penury. They both took service with the government and worked long years as accountants. Both were imprisoned for debts. They were unfortunate in their marriages, and consequently looked for love elsewhere. Both unsuccessfully sought a government position in the New World, and having been denied it, remained in Spain and penned their masterpieces. These personal reverses were fortunate for Spanish letters, since it is unlikely that either would have created his great novel had he obtained a position in the Indies. Both composed their chief works at a mature age and poured their reasoned philosophy of life into their novels. They published their masterworks in two parts, and the first part was continued by imitators who hid under pseudonyms. These spurious continuations aroused them to compose the authentic second part, in which they satirized their imitators.[43] Their masterpieces were remarkable successes as measured by fame, but not by monetary return. They were equally unlucky in the choice of patrons for their works, receiving little or no aid from the men whose names they immortalized on the title pages of their books.

But here the parallelism ceases. Mateo Alemán was able to

emigrate to Mexico on the second attempt, and there found the happiness he had sought in vain in his homeland; Cervantes resigned himself to staying at home, and posterity is the richer for his sacrifice. Though there are similarities of form and content in their novels, the basic attitude expressed toward life is diametrically opposed, for Cervantes was able to smile in the face of misfortune, whereas Alemán could only scowl.

A theory frequently advanced regarding the relationship of Alemán and Cervantes is that there was some ill feeling between them. It has been claimed that the two great novelists met either in the Royal Prison of Seville or in Italy, and their misunderstanding stemmed from this meeting. Modern research has shown, however, that Alemán and Cervantes could not have become acquainted in either of these places, for they were in debtor's prison at different times, and Alemán did not go to Italy. Of course they could have met elsewhere, but no definite proof of hostility between them has been advanced so far.

The facts of their relationship are as follows: Ginés de Pasamonte, a minor picaresque character in *Don Quixote* (Part I, Chapter 22), is patterned after the protagonist of Alemán's novel. Like Guzmán, Ginés is a famous thief who has been captured and condemned to the galleys, where he plans to write his life history. On his way to the galleys, Ginés, like Guzmán, has an adventure at an inn, but it is merely alluded to, not developed, so there is no way of knowing if it is similar to Guzmán's. Here ends the resemblance between the characters, for Ginés and the other prisoners with him are set free by Don Quixote and do not end up in the galleys. If it is assumed that Cervantes was acquainted with Alemán's life, it is possible to draw another analogy, this time between the picaresque novelist and Don Quixote. The immortal knight's action of freeing the galley prisoners is quite similar to Alemán's liberation of the inmates of the jail of Usagre in 1583. It is curious that Cervantes fuses, intentionally or accidentally, a literary reminiscence with an actual episode in Alemán's life.

Several years later, Cervantes praised *Guzmán de Alfarache* in his novelette *La ilustre fregona* (*The Illustrious Kitchenmaid*). As far as is known, Alemán made no reference in his writings to

Cervantes or to his works.[44] It is known that he took *Don Quixote* with him to Mexico and thought highly enough of it to request the return of his copy when it was confiscated. Further study is needed to determine if Alemán and Cervantes were really enemies.

CHAPTER 2

General Considerations on Guzmán de Alfarache

I *Brief Definition and History of the Picaresque Novel*

THE picaresque novel begins with the anonymous Spanish novel *Lazarillo de Tormes,*[1] which appeared in three different editions in 1554. Although remote antecedents of the picaresque novel can be sought in Classical and medieval literature, the short *Lazarillo* sets the pattern for the species. The genre has been cultivated in several countries from the middle of the sixteenth century to the present; consequently, its form has varied somewhat with period, nation, and individual taste. Certain features, however, are characteristic of the picaresque novel.[2]

(1) The protagonist is a picaro or rogue—an individual related to three other literary types: the wanderer, the have-not, and the jester. The wanderer who roves from place to place in search of adventure is apparently almost as old as narrative literature itself; the Classical prototype is Odysseus. The have-not first emerged as an important literary character during the Renaissance in the so-called "anatomies of roguery." These books portrayed the low life of beggars, criminals, and ruffians. In Spain this kind of literature is best represented by Carlos García's *La desordenada codicia de los bienes ajenos* (*The Lawless Covetousness of other People's Possessions* [Paris, 1619]), although the low-lifer had made his appearance much earlier in Fernando de Rojas' *Celestina* (1499) and in Francisco Delicado's *La lozana andaluza* (*The Exuberant Andalusian Woman*), composed in 1524. In England the first anatomy of roguery is John Awdeley's *Fraternitye of Vacabondes* (1561). The jester is an-

other important type in Renaissance literature. A relative of the fool in Latin comedy, he is a stock figure in medieval stories. The most famous jestbook hero of the Renaissance is the German Till Eulenspiegel. The picaro is an errant person, like the wanderer; he often begs or steals a meager sustenance, like the have-not; and he loves to display his wit in knavish tricks, like the jester. But the rogue goes beyond all these types. Unlike them, he does not remain static, but continually grows and develops.

The rogue starts out in life with the cards stacked against him. His parents are unsavory individuals who not only fail to teach him moral values, but do not even attempt to dissimulate their own gross failings. Usually the family suffers economic want and the future picaro, often an orphan, must shift for himself at an early age. His first contacts with society jolt him, but the inexperienced boy soon learns how to defend himself. With time the rogue aspires to a better economic and social position. His environment seems to conspire against him at every turn, but the picaro struggles undaunted, using cheats and wiles to further his ambition. He feels very much alone in his battle with the world.

The picaro is the first character of humble station to become the protagonist of a work of fiction. Lowly characters had appeared frequently in literature, usually as comic figures, but always in a subordinate capacity. The leading roles had been reserved for noble personages. The other genres cultivated in Spain during the Renaissance—the book of chivalry, the sentimental novel, the pastoral romance, the Moorish novel—all had protagonists of gentle birth. The emergence of the rogue as a hero, or rather, an anti-hero, was an important step in the development of the modern novel.

(2) The point of view of the picaresque novel is autobiographical. The author identifies himself with his humble protagonist and describes the world from the latter's peculiar angle of vision, that of the underdog. There is no pretense of objective description of reality. While the idealistic genres such as the book of chivalry and the pastoral novel emphasize the more beautiful aspects of life (love, for example), the picaresque novel dwells on the more sordid (hunger, for instance).

(3) The picaro usually writes with a double purpose: to amuse and to instruct at the same time. The humor is furnished by the rogue's description of his knaveries and his discomfitures. The didactic elements can take the form either of a satire on society's ills, or of direct moralizing. The picaro normally pens his autobiography when a mature man; therefore he possesses critical insight into the problems he treats.

(4) The rogue ordinarily serves several masters and his wanderings bring him into contact with people of many occupations. His commentaries on the different social classes are generally satirical or ironic.

(5) The picaresque novel has an episodic structure. The only apparent unity in the series of adventures is the developing personality of the rogue. The autobiographical form of narration presupposes that the relator is still alive at the end of his story; consequently, the novel is left open to further adventures. A large proportion of picaresque novels have sequels not written by the original authors.

As was stated earlier, all of the essential characteristics of the picaresque novel are found in the first specimen of the genre, *Lazarillo de Tormes.* Lázaro is the son of a lowly thief and a woman of loose morals. At an early age his mother entrusts him to a blind beggar, who teaches the boy how to get along in the world. He subsequently serves an avaricious priest and a proud squire. While living with his first three masters, Lazarillo's major preoccupation is to ward off starvation; the tricks he employs to get food always cause humorous situations and often lead to drubbings. The vagabond later works for several other masters, but not all these episodes are fully developed. *Lazarillo* was banned by the Inquisition in 1559 because of its irreverent satire of the clergy, but its continued popularity caused Philip II to commission an expurgated edition which appeared in 1573. An anonymous sequel to *Lazarillo* was printed in Antwerp in 1555. It is an uninspired work in which Lazarillo is transformed into a tuna and has extravagant and tiresome adventures in the bottom of the ocean. Another continuation was published in Paris in 1620 by Juan de Luna. This entertaining novel frequently satirizes the clergy and the Inquisition, and is racier in tone than most Spanish works. Juan Cortés de Tolosa's *Lazarillo de Man-*

zanares (Madrid, 1620) is not a sequel to *Lazarillo de Tormes*, in spite of the similarity of title. Some of this rogue's amusing adventures parallel those of previous picaresque works.

The second picaresque novel published in Spain was Alemán's *Guzmán de Alfarache* (1599). Its structure is modeled on that of *Lazarillo*, but Alemán accomplishes his social criticism by moralizing rather than by satire. *Guzmán* presents a greater variety of adventures than *Lazarillo* and gives a deeper analysis of its protagonist's character. The extraordinary acceptance of *Guzmán* prompted the Valencian Juan Martí to publish a mediocre continuation in 1602; the genuine second part appeared in 1604. The next Spanish picaresque novel is *La pícara Justina* (1605), whose protagonist is, as the title indicates, a woman. The action of this novel is extremely weak; the work is saved only by its picturesque language and abstruse satire.

The only Spanish novel of roguery that rivals *Lazarillo* and *Guzmán* in artistry is Francisco de Quevedo's *El Buscón* (*The Sharper*). Although first published in 1626, it was probably written over twenty years earlier. Many incidents in *El Buscón* are based on Alemán's novel. Quevedo's originality consists of his style rather than the action and characterization; *El Buscón* represents the ultimate in caricature. Quevedo distorts reality almost to the point of destroying it, yet he conveys a clear impression of that reality. *El Buscón* is similar to *Lazarillo* in its conciseness and density.

Vicente Espinel's *Marcos de Obregón* (1618) is usually included among Spanish picaresque novels, although the protagonist is not a complete rogue but rather the author's loquacious *alter ego*. This tiresome book is full of moralistic digressions and autobiographical allusions. Another novel that can be considered picaresque only in a broad sense is *Alonso, mozo de muchos amos* (*Alonso, the Servant of Many Masters*), published by Jerónimo de Alcalá Yáñez in two parts in 1624 and 1626. Like Marcos de Obregón, Alonso is more of a self-righteous busybody than a picaro. *Alonso* contains many interpolated stories and anecdotes, as does *Guzmán*. Several novels of Alonso Jerónimo de Salas Barbadillo and Alonso del Castillo Solórzano have knavish protagonists, but do not possess the other characteristics of the picaresque genre. Luis Vélez de Guevara's *El diablo cojuelo* (*The Little Lame Devil*), published in 1641, presents a satirical picture of society's vices, but without the picaresque framework.

The classical Spanish picaresque novel comes to an end in 1646 with the publication of Estebanillo González' *Vida* (*Life*). It appears that this book is largely autobiographical, although little is known about González. The narrator takes great delight in describing his coarse tricks, which he plays in several European countries, but gives no attention to social criticism. With the loss of ethical intention, the picaresque genre becomes simply a novel of adventures. The true novel of roguery was not to reappear in Spain until the middle of the twentieth century.

The Spanish picaresque novel became available in the rest of Europe within a relatively short time. *Lazarillo* was translated into French in 1560 and appeared in England in 1568. The other popular picaresque works were rendered into English, French, German, and Italian during the seventeenth century. However, in most countries the genre was not imitated for many years.

The first picaresque novels to appear outside of Spain were written in Germany.[3] In 1615, the Jesuit Aegidius Albertinus printed a free translation of *Guzmán de Alfarache* (containing elements from Martí's continuation), and added to it a second part which was really an original sequel. A third part of *Guzmán* was published in 1626 by the pseudonymous author Martinus Freudenhold. Both of these sequels to Alemán's work are excessively preoccupied with moralizing and have little aesthetic merit. The next cultivator of the picaresque, contrariwise, wrote the best German novel of the seventeenth century. Hans Jacob Christoffel von Grimmelshausen penned several picaresque novels, of which the most famous is *Simplicissimus* (*The Simpleton*), published in 1668. This is the story of a boy who, growing up in solitude, is at first incredibly simple, later learns enough to fall upon bad ways, but finally repents. Simplicius' wanderings permit Grimmelshausen to portray the coarseness and corruption of contemporary society, which is placed against the background of the Thirty Years' War. At the end the picaro reflects on his sinful ways and becomes a hermit.

Perhaps the most artistic continuation of the Spanish picaresque tradition, and its closest imitation, is *Gil Blas de Santillane*

(1715-1735), by Alain René Lesage. It is one of the better French novels of the eighteenth century.[4] Gil Blas is a Spaniard, the setting is in Spain, and many incidents are patterned after Spanish models. In the prologue Gil Blas affirms the typically picaresque intention of mingling profit with pleasure, but in his entertaining narration the interest in adventure obscures the satirical perspective. About three quarters of the way through the work, the protagonist undergoes a conversion while in prison (this spiritual rebirth is similar to that which Guzmán de Alfarache experiences on the galley), and thereafter leads a correct life. During the post-picaresque stage of his life, Gil Blas earns a title of nobility, acquires a country house, is happily married, and has two children.

The picaresque genre did not become entirely acclimatized in England, where only certain ingredients of the formula were accepted. Daniel Defoe's *Moll Flanders* (1722), for example, coincides with the picaresque narratives in that it is the episodic autobiography of a roguish figure; but Moll recounts her adventures in a mechanical sort of way, without the combination of humor and ethical purpose that characterizes the pícaro. Moll's sole motivation is the desire for lucre; she does not exhibit the pícaro's delight in his rogueries for their own sake. Perhaps the Englishman who came closest to the continental tradition of the picaresque novel was Tobias Smollett. His *Roderick Random* (1748) and *Ferdinand Count Fathom* (1753) commence in the roguish mode of the endless wanderings related autobiographically. But the last third of *Roderick Random* and the second half of *Ferdinand* change into sentimental romances—a type of narrative most uncongenial to the picaresque spirit. Henry Fielding's *Tom Jones* (1749) likewise embodies some roguish elements but lacks the fundamental traits of the pseudo-autobiography, the protagonist who relishes trickery, the world view typical of the outsider, etc. What these English writers do is to choose certain techniques and attitudes of the picaresque novel and adapt them to their own times and tastes.

The roguish tradition was forgotten in Spain during the eighteenth and nineteenth centuries. (Diego de Torres Villarroel's *Vida* [1743-1758], occasionally called a picaresque novel, is simply an autobiography written in jocose style.) In contrast, the first novel produced in Spanish America belongs to the picaresque genre. The Mexican José Joaquín Fernández de Lizardi published his *Periquillo sarniento* (*The Itching Parrot*) in 1816. Unfortunately, the novel reflects an excessive absorption in the description of customs and manners, and is marred by a plethora of moralistic and didactic digressions. Like *Guzmán de Alfarache* and other Spanish novels of roguery, *Periquillo* contains interpolated stories. In his second picaresque novel, *Don Catrín de la Fachenda,* published posthumously in 1832, Lizardi avoids the defect of open preaching, but does not make his character psychologically convincing. Unlike the traditional picaresque novel, which has an open ending, both of Lizardi's works are brought to a close by the death of the protagonist. Over a hundred years later, in 1938, there appeared another Mexican version of the novel of roguery. José Rubén Romero's *La vida inútil de Pito Pérez* (*The Useless Life of Pito Pérez*) incorporates numerous picaresque features. Pito wanders from one small provincial town to another, having amusing adventures with a series of masters. *Pito Pérez* is not only anticlerical, like *Lazarillo de Tormes,* but also anti-Christian. Like his predecessor Don Catrín, Pito dies unrepentant as a consequence of his dissipated life.

The tradition of the near-picaresque novel continued elsewhere during the nineteenth and twentieth centuries. A remote French descendant of Lazarillo de Tormes is found in Julien Sorel, the hero of Stendhal's *Le Rouge et le Noir* (*The Red and the Black*), published in 1830. Later derivations appear in William Thackeray's *Barry Lyndon* (1844) and Mark Twain's great American classic, *Huckleberry Finn* (1884). The picaresque form has been adapted to the exigencies of the modern novel in Saul Bellow's *The Adventures of Augie March* (1953), Joyce Cary's *The Horse's Mouth* (1944), and the German Thomas Mann's *Felix Krull* (1954). The last two novels offer the peculiarity of making the pseudo-rogue an artist.

The picaresque genre is still alive today in the country of its origin. In 1944, almost on the four hundredth anniversary of his initial appearance, the first Spanish rogue recommenced his adventures in Camilo José Cela's *Nuevas andanzas y desventuras de Lazarillo de Tormes* (*New Wanderings and Misfortunes of Lazarillo de Tormes*). The new Lazarillo is quite a different character from his namesake and the other classic pícaros. He feels a genuine tenderness toward his fellowman and is remarkably sensitive to such spiritual things as the beauties of nature. Another novelty is that Lazarillo is not tempted by the thought of social or economic gains; he is perfectly happy to serve for room and board and little more. Although Cela's novel has occasional moments of indelicacy and of horror, the predominant tone is almost poetic, because Lázaro describes the shortcomings of his fellow creatures with infinite understanding. The *New Wanderings of Lazarillo* is a worthy successor to the great picaresque novels of Spain's Golden Age.

II *The Plot of* Guzmán

Although the action of *Guzmán de Alfarache* will be examined in detail in Chapters 4-6, a summary of the plot is given here to facilitate reference.

Guzmán is born in Seville, the illegitimate offspring of a Genoese usurer and a Spanish prostitute. When the boy is twelve, his father dies, leaving the family in poor financial condition. Guzmán decides to shift for himself and sets out for Genoa, where his paternal relatives live. His misadventures begin when he is served nearly-hatched eggs at an inn. Later in the day, at another inn, he eats mule flesh for veal. Subsequently, Guzmán is mistaken for a thief and is arrested and beaten. A traveling companion relates the story of *Ozmín and Daraja.*

After serving as a stableboy at an inn, Guzmán moves on to Madrid, where he joins the ranks of the pícaros and plies their typical trade of carrying baskets. Later he works for a cook, but is dismissed as a result of seeing his master's wife naked. Returning to his carrier job, Guzmán steals a large sum and goes to Toledo. There he buys smart clothes and engages in erotic adventures, all unsuccessful. He joins a company of soldiers headed for Italy and soon squanders his ill-gotten money. Obliged to seek a master, he supports an army captain for a time, but is discharged on arrival in Genoa. The boy contacts his father's family, but is maltreated because of his poverty. The rogue hurriedly leaves Genoa and begs his way to Rome. In the Eternal City he joins a fraternity of beggars and learns how to produce false cankers that arouse pity in almsgivers. A compassionate Cardinal takes Guzmán into his service. The indulgent prelate tolerates many of the boy's knavish tricks, but dismisses him when he becomes an inveterate gambler. Guzmán then plays the part of buffoon for the French Ambassador in Rome. In the latter's house the picaro hears the story of *Dorido and Clorinia*, which closes Part I.

At the beginning of Part II, Guzmán serves the French Ambassador as page and pander. One night he plays a prank on some dinner guests and the story of *Don Luis de Castro* is related in order to appease them. The picaro's activities as a go-between cause him to be punished by a chaste lady, who makes him spend a night in a stenchy nook. A few days later, when he is about his pandering, a pig runs between Guzmán's legs and carries him on its back through filth-covered streets. As a result, the picaro becomes an object of ridicule and has to leave Rome. In Siena, a friend named Sayavedra impersonates Guzmán and makes off with his luggage. While journeying to Florence the rogue meets Sayavedra, who implores his pardon and becomes his servant. In Bologna Guzmán denounces an accomplice in the larceny, but the thief has powerful connections and gets his accuser imprisoned for slander.

After his release from jail, Guzmán cheats at cards with Sayavedra's collusion and wins much money. They depart for Milan, where Guzmán defrauds a usurer of several thousand crowns. He triumphantly enters Genoa, claiming to be a gentleman named Don Juan de Guzmán. The relatives who repudiated the picaro seven years before now fawn on him, but Guzmán takes revenge by robbing them. He sails for Spain. During the voyage a storm overtakes the ship and Sayavedra casts himself into the sea. To console Guzmán's feigned sorrow, the story of *Bonifacio and Dorotea* is related.

Guzmán disembarks in Barcelona. At a tavern in Saragossa he hears the statutes of an order of fools. Later the rogue is twice duped by streetwalkers. Proceeding to Madrid, Guzmán buys a house and becomes a usurer. He marries the daughter of a moneylender. She ruins Guzmán financially and dies soon after. The picaro resolves to study for the priesthood in Alcalá de Henares, in order to assure himself an easy livelihood. Shortly before his ordainment Guzmán falls hopelessly in love and marries again. When bad times come, the calloused rogue prostitutes his wife and achieves momentary economic well-being. The couple moves to Seville and Guzmán's mother, now a procuress, panders for her daughter-in-law. After his wife runs away to Italy with a galley captain, Guzmán resorts to petty theft and swindling. The law finally catches up with him and he is condemned to row six years on a galley; when he attempts to escape from prison in disguise, his sentence is increased to life. On board the galley he repents of his past life and denounces a mutiny. The novel concludes with the promise that Guzmán will receive his freedom.

III *The History of* Guzmán *Criticism*

Students of the Spanish picaresque novel are agreed that *Guzmán de Alfarache* is the most important example of the genre; Mateo Alemán's masterpiece is universally considered the picaresque novel par excellence. This does not mean that *Guzmán* is generally held to be a more artistic work than *Lazarillo de Tormes,* the prototype of the species. There seems to be conformity of opinion that, page for page, the anonymous short novel is of higher quality than *Guzmán,* in spite of the fact that its last chapters are only incomplete sketches. Indeed, most readers choose Francisco de Quevedo's *El Buscón,* the third and last great Spanish picaresque novel, over *Guzmán.* However, Alemán's work is regarded as the quintessential example of the genre, because it is more complex, thematically speaking, than the other two novels. It offers a richness of thought and multiplicity of interpretations not possible in the short pages of *Lazarillo de Tormes* and *El Buscón.* The greater length of *Guzmán* is largely responsible for its superior complexity.

Like all masterpieces, *Guzmán de Alfarache* contains an ambiguity that permits different generations to interpret it in diverse ways. *Guzmán*'s ambiguousness consists in the contrast between the protagonist's roguish life and the moralistic manner in which he narrates his escapades. There is a conflict between the narrator's obvious delight in describing his past knaveries and his profuse strictures of immoral conduct.[5]

No criticism of *Guzmán*'s time has been preserved. In early seventeenth century Spain, opinions about literary works were usually expressed orally at informal gatherings and were seldom committed to print. The only existing comments about the novel are the encomiums of Alemán's friends (printed at the beginning of Parts I and II), the imprimaturs of censors, and the observations of translators.[6] These bits of information are of little value, for they merely repeat the commonplace formula applied by such persons to many Golden Age works: to wit, that the book in question satisfies the Classical precept of combining a moral lesson with entertainment. Another piece of evidence that better reveals what Alemán's contemporaries saw in *Guzmán* is the common reference to it as *El pícaro* ("The Rogue"). In bills of sale, bills of lading, and other documents, the novel is referred to by this epithet. Alemán himself complained that his book was known only as "The Picaro" (see Section VI below). This is eloquent testimony that the seventeenth century Spaniard enjoyed *Guzmán* for its adventures, not for its profound thought. The same was to be true of *Don Quixote*. English tastes of the period ran along similar lines.[7]

The eighteenth century, the period of the Enlightenment, was uniform in its evaluation of Alemán's novel. It regarded the adventures as highly diverting, but condemned the moralistic digressions. Alain René Lesage, the author of *Gil Blas de Santillane,* published in 1732 a French adaptation of *Guzmán,* in which he omitted the "superfluous moralizations." This shortened version was later rendered into English. Leandro Fernández de Moratín, the outstanding Spanish dramatist of the century, also undertook a revision of *Guzmán,* eliminating the digressions.[8] Gregorio Mayans y Siscar, one of the most erudite Spaniards of the eighteenth century, praised *Guzmán* in his *Specimen Bibliothecae Hispano-Majansianae* (1753), but criticized the prolixity of its moralizations.

Many nineteenth century critics saw an irreconcilable dichotomy between Guzmán's adventures and his moralizations. They claimed that the digressions were to counterbalance the bad example of Guzmán's actions, and that Alemán included them to save his book from ecclesiastical censure. This theory is naïve, because the Church never reproved picaresque adventures that did not fringe on heterodoxy. Moreover, clerical censors would not accept any amount of moralizing as compensation for heretical material—the offensive passages had to be removed. In spite of its unacceptability, the "Inquisition theory" still has followers today. By way of contrast, one nineteenth century critic, Eustaquio Fernández de Navarrete,[9] had the perspicacity to see that the moralizations are an integral part of *Guzmán de Alfarache,* given the state of mind of the protagonist when he writes. Guzmán relates his autobiography not only to entertain, but also to instruct the reader; the rogue desires to help others avoid the snares into which he has fallen.

In 1937 Miguel Herrero[10] gave new direction to *Guzmán* criticism by affirming that the picaresque novel is a pseudo-ascetic product. Herrero compared the structure of *Guzmán* to that of a sermon. A religious discourse consists primarily of moralizing, with a sprinkling of stories and anecdotes to illustrate and enliven the ethical lesson; *Guzmán* inverts the proportions, making the moralizations subordinate to the adventures. Angel Valbuena Prat[11] subsequently reiterated that the ascetic part of *Guzmán* should not be separated from the picaresque. Alemán conceived the work on two planes, the moral and the novelistic, and they should be considered together. An outstanding tenet of Valbuena's theory is that in *Guzmán* there is a constant struggle between temptation and the call of God's grace.

This later position is the point of departure for the monograph of Moreno Báez on the "lesson and meaning" of *Guzmán.*[12] Moreno Báez believes that Alemán's novel was elaborated with the constant preoccupation of expounding the doctrine set forth by the Council of Trent regarding sin and the salvation of man by his faith and works. By virtue of his free will and of God's grace, the picaro finds his way to Heaven in spite of his transgressions. Moreno Báez' procedure is first to state Catholic doctrine and then to examine *Guzmán,* looking for bits of proof to fit into his preconceived pattern. This critic concerns himself almost exclusively with the digressions, neglecting the work's narrative values.

Moreno Báez' thesis has been rejected by many critics. Gonzalo Sobejano,[13] for example, has noted that *Guzmán* is an educational, rather than a purely religious, novel. The reader is taught to lead an orderly life, fleeing from the bad example set by the picaro and by the society in which he lives. For Sobejano, the originality of Alemán's novel lies in its criticism of many social classes. He also points out, quite correctly, that there is greater emphasis on religion in Part II; the Guzmán who narrates Part I is merely a man who has learned his lesson and regrets not having been virtuous, whereas the relator of the continuation is a penitent anguished by the thought of the moral abyss into which he has slipped.

Summing up the history of the evolution of *Guzmán* criticism, two points stand out: (1) readers from the seventeenth century to the present have received enormous pleasure from the picaresque adventures; (2) all discussion about the novel's value and intention revolves around the moralistic digressions. Modern critics have restored the moralizations to their proper place as an organic component of *Guzmán*. But in so doing, they have greatly exaggerated the importance of the digressions at the expense of the action, which is always the essence of fiction. The fact remains that *Guzmán* is first and foremost a *novel,* not an ascetic treatise. The great majority of its pages are devoted to the relation of humorous and ingenious adventures. It is true that a significant moral and religious lesson is to be learned in *Guzmán,* just as in many novels. But much more importantly, it is a very amusing work of entertainment. Only by ignoring *Guzmán*'s narrative value can it be maintained that its primary purpose is to illustrate the doctrines of original sin, free will, and grace. These religious elements are incidental topics, not the principal concern. Had Alemán intended to compose a religious tract, he would not have chosen the novel as a vehicle for his expression, and he certainly would not have devoted most of his space to roguish tricks.

IV *The Structure of* Guzmán de Alfarache

The structure of *Guzmán de Alfarache* is quite different from that of previous Spanish novels, although there are scattered precedents for all its components.[14] The skeleton of the work is composed of Guzmán's autobiographical narration. The account of his roguish adventures is the fundamental substance of the novel; for this reason it belongs to the picaresque genre.

This portion of the novel consists of reminiscences of the mature Guzmán, writing from the galley, about the more outstanding events of his life.

Accompanying the relation of the picaro's adventures are the moralizations and didactic considerations interpolated by the worldly-wise and disenchanted narrator. These digressions constitute a running commentary on the action. Guzmán's experiences always provide the point of departure for these considerations; no digressions are intercalated gratuitously—all have an organic relation to the knaveries of the immature rogue. Sometimes the moralization serves as an introduction to an adventure, building up suspense for it. Other times the digression is an epilogue that draws conclusions of a general nature from the episode immediately preceding.

There are several types of digressions, ranging from the full-blown sermon to the single aphoristic sentence. These discourses are introduced in diverse fashions. They may take the form of a monologue by the boy Guzmán ("I began to think with my selfe, sure, this good old man is my kinsman . . ." [*Rogue,* I, 187]),[15] or a monologue inserted by the mature narrator ("I was but young, I did not dive to the bottome of his drift, I only lookt upon . . . the outward appearance" [*ibid.*]). On occasion the protagonist is really two persons who converse with each other ("Here (*Guzman*) thou shalt see what a kinde of thing Honour is . . . Tell me I pray, who is that that gives honour unto some . . . Tell me once more I pray . . . Thou hast put too hard a taske upon mee . . . But I shall tell thee . . ." [I, 122-23]), or he debates with an imaginary person, presumably the disagreeing reader ("Shall I here say any thing unto you concerning this point? Mee thinkes I heare you say, No . . ." [II, 283]).

To illustrate the digressions, Guzmán interpolates many exempla, or short moral tales. His procedure is directly analogical to that of the preacher who inserts anecdotes into his sermon with the twofold purpose of arousing his audience's interest and of teaching a moral or practical lesson. Like the repertory of the adroit preacher, Guzmán's collection of anecdotes encompasses everything from the amusing tale to the allegorical story, including the yarn from folklore, the personal experience, the mythological narrative, the Classical apologue, and the animal fable.

Many of these stories come from written sources, others were undoubtedly taken from oral reports. The tales are encrusted in the digressions much like bits of glass in a mosaic. Since they are illustrations of the moralizations, the stories are twice removed from the main action, but they still have an indirect relation to it. Many proverbs and ballads are included in *Guzmán*, and they serve a purpose similar to that of the anecdotes, illuminating and adorning the digressions.

Completely separate from the other major elements are the interpolated novelettes. They provide a contrast to the picaresque adventures by shifting momentarily the reader's attention to a different set of characters. The four novelettes are truly small jewels hidden away in the pages of Guzmán's adventures. They make the structure more complex.

With very few exceptions (i.e., the autobiography of Sayavedra in II, ii, 4; the dialogue in II, ii, 5-6, where Guzmán robs a Milanese merchant; the slave's letter in II, iii, 7), the entire novel is narrated by the protagonist. However, Alemán avoids monotony by utilizing different styles in accord with the various types of narration. For describing Guzmán's adventures, he employs a simple, direct, and agile style—a colloquial type of language full of idioms, proverbs, paronomasias, and puns. The construction is usually straightforward, although complicated at times by the use of zeugma. The vocabulary is amazingly rich, containing terms from many areas: nautical and juridical words, phrases from gambling, hunting, fencing, and other sports and games. Alemán does not introduce neologisms from Latin, but is "demonstrably addicted to Italianisms."[16] In the digressions, on the other hand, he uses a more rhetorical and florid style. Reiterations, parallel and symmetrical constructions, hair-splitting definitions, emblematic images—all these devices are found in his moralizations. The anecdotes, in contrast, are often related in a popular diction reproducing slang and incorrect speech, to communicate the flavor of the uneducated speaker.

The circumstances under which Mateo Alemán wrote Part I of *Guzmán* were quite different from those under which he composed Part II. He had many years to meditate about the first part of his novel, publishing it at the age of fifty-two. The final version of the continuation, contrariwise, was drafted in less than a year and a half, and perhaps in only a matter of months. These conditions are naturally reflected in the two parts of the novel. Part I has better balance between the four elements of adventures, digressions, anecdotes, and novelettes. In the first part there is a predominance of action, and the digressions are evenly distributed (Chapters 3-4 of Book ii constitute an exception, for they are largely digressive). The anecdotes are spread out too, and the novelettes are strategically placed at the end of Books i and iii. A good example of the structure of Part I of *Guzmán* is furnished by the first chapter. The protagonist begins by telling about his father, who he claims has been calumniated. The chief subject of the chapter is a mock defense by Guzmán of his progenitor. To clear his father's reputation, the rogue digresses against slanderers, venal scriveners and judges, and dishonest merchants. Shorter criticisms are directed to effeminate men (such as his father) and women who spend excessive time beautifying themselves. To drive home the points of his digressions, Guzmán intercalates three different types of anecdotes: one about an artist who includes many irrelevant objects in a painting of a horse, hoping for extra pay (an example of how people exaggerate the truth); another about a peasant who saw a statue of Justice placed high above a building and thought it was out of his reach (an illustration of how corruption perverts justice); and an allegory about a monster who typified the vices of the Italian people.

The structure of Part II lacks the symmetry and balance of Part I. The first four chapters of the continuation contain no action, being composed entirely of anecdotes, digressions, and a novelette. Elsewhere too the moralizations and anecdotes tend to be bunched, rather than fitting in smoothly with the adventures. The principal action is likewise concentrated in separate chapters. The result is that Part II does not flow evenly, but progresses by fits and starts.

Like all Baroque art, the structure of *Guzmán de Alfarache* contains an inner order, in spite of its outward appearance of derangement. Guzmán's adventures constitute the main framework of the novel and offer specific examples of human conduct. The digressions are grafted onto the adventures and relate them to the universal patterns of mankind's behavior. The adventures are concrete, while the digressions are general. The numerous anecdotes that enliven the narration are other specific illustrations of man's nature. The novelettes are independent interludes that analyze other aspects of human conduct than those examined in the picaresque adventures, and they present different types of characters.

V *The Indebtedness of* Guzmán *to* Lazarillo

The earliest known editions of *Lazarillo de Tormes,* the first picaresque novel, are of 1554. It immediately gained great popularity. However, almost half a century elapsed before the picaresque vein was again cultivated in Spain—by the publication of *Guzmán* in 1599. The reason for the lack of descendants of *Lazarillo* is not hard to find. *Lazarillo* has a predominately anticlerical tone; five of its seven chapters are chiefly satires of different levels of the ecclesiastical order, and the remaining chapters contain barbed allusions to the clergy. In view of the historical circumstances prevailing in Spain in the second half of the sixteenth century—the kings who conceived as their principal mission the propagation of Catholicism, the enormous power of the Inquisition, the ideals of the Counter-Reformation, the strict censorship of books by the Church—it is not surprising that no writer was foolish enough to continue the tendencies of the author of *Lazarillo,* who dared not reveal his identity. The first work of the picaresque genre was placed on the Index of prohibited books in 1559, just a few years after its appearance. It was clear, therefore, that *Lazarillo de Tormes* could not be the ideological model for a new literary species—this pattern would have to be furnished by an arch-Catholic work, such as that of Alemán. *Lazarillo*'s influence was not ideological, but structural: all subsequent picaresque novels were to imitate its external form and occasionally some of its more innocuous episodes. The anticlerical tendency, although extremely fecund at this time in Italy and France, was to die stillborn in Spain.[17]

As far as a religious "message" is concerned, *Guzmán de Alfarache* must be considered a refutation of *Lazarillo de Tormes,* not a continuation. The unknown author satirizes the clergy; Alemán exalts it. The priesthood is the only profession (besides the kingship) to be constantly extolled in *Guzmán*. At one point Alemán goes so far as to make a direct reply to *Lazarillo*, converting its most despicable character—the priest of Maqueda—into the noblest character in *Guzmán*: the Roman Cardinal who cares for the rogue as if he were his own prodigal son.

Mateo Alemán's imitations of *Lazarillo* fall into two large categories: generic characteristics and specific details. As for basic similarities, the two novels coincide in their dual purpose: that of entertaining and instructing at the same time. Recent criticism too often has lost sight of the first of these aims, which was surely meant to be the more important. The simple fact is that the picaresque novel is designed to produce abundant laughter in its reader; most of its space is devoted to adventures of a humorous nature (or to entertaining tales and novelettes in *Guzmán*). Both novels contain much slapstick humor; *Lazarillo* also includes much verbal comedy (irony)—an element generally lacking in *Guzmán* except in the first two chapters, which are inspired by *Lazarillo*.

A fundamental trait that Alemán's protagonist shares with Lázaro is his peculiarly picaresque vision of the world.[18] The pícaro does not see mankind objectively, but with a jaundiced view; it is as though he contemplates society with special prisms that filter out the good. He is ever alert to man's imperfections, but rarely sees his positive qualities. This prejudiced view is to a considerable extent the result of the inferior social position into which the rogue was born. His parents' lack of status is a powerful determining factor in the life of the pícaro.

The Spanish rogue narrates the story of his life to an interested listener, variously referred to as "Your Excellency" (*Lazarillo*) or the "Curious Reader" (*Guzmán*). The intimacy achieved through this familiar treatment is in accord with the personal nature of many of the revelations the protagonist is to make about his family and himself. A peculiar narrative point of view is used to relate the pícaro's autobiography. The narrator is a mature man who recalls his adventures of younger years. Thus the protagonist has a double perspective on his life: that of the naïve waif and that of the experienced older man. The contrast between these two visions is a continual source of humor. A good example recounted by Lazarillo is his thinking that a corpse was being carried to the house of his master, the squire, because a mourning wife complained that her dead husband was going to the dark and dreary house where people neither eat nor drink. The perspective of time not only allows the rogues to see the humorous side of painful experiences, but also to meditate upon their universal significance.

There are also important differences between the narrative points of view of *Lazarillo* and *Guzmán.* In *Lazarillo* there is a third point of view, in addition to those of the boy who has the adventures and the man who relates them. This third person is the author, whose vision of the world does not coincide with either one of the others. The best example occurs in the last chapter of the novel, where the protagonist pretends to believe that his wife is virtuous, but gives convincing evidence to the contrary. It is as though the author places himself behind Lázaro and winks at the reader, telling him not to believe what he says. The effect is a loss of verisimilitude, a breaking of dramatic illusion, as when in the theater a character jokes about the play itself, reminding the viewer that he is watching the performance of an artistic fiction, not a real event. This means that Lazarillo is not a character with his own psychology, because at any time the author can stick out his head and tell the reader that Lázaro is only a puppet. In other words, the creator of Lazarillo has sacrificed the psychology of his character to his satirical purpose. Mateo Alemán avoids this problem by identifying himself completely with the narrator, making him his spokesman. The identification is so complete, particularly in Part II of *Guzmán,* that the author attributes numerous autobiographical details to his creature.

Lazarillo and *Guzmán* have the same episodic structure, as the protagonist wanders from one adventure to another. A significant part of the action in both novels is based on incidents from folklore or from the Italian *novella.* Much of the borrowed material has to do with ingenious thefts. Often in the history of the novel, such an emphasis on action is accompanied by a sacrifice in character development. This is true of *Lazarillo,* where the protagonist is not fully developed psychologically. Mateo Alemán, on the other hand, delineates most carefully the psychology of Guzmán, who has surprisingly little in common with Lazarillo. It should be noted, however, that Lázaro's masters are much more individualized than Guzmán's. In the gallery of personages that appear in *Guzmán de Alfarache,* none stands out so sharply as *Lazarillo*'s beggar, priest of Maqueda, or squire. With the exceptions of the Italian Cardinal and the French Ambassador, the faces of Guzmán's masters tend to be rather expressionless.

There are numerous less basic, more formal types of coincidences between the two novels. Lazarillo de Tormes adopts as his cognomen the name of the river on which he was born; Guzmán takes as his surname the appellation of the place where he was conceived, Alfarache. The protagonists' names serve as titles of the works. Lazarillo leaves home because his mother, a widow, considers herself unable to continue supporting him. Guzmán also states that he was forced to leave home, although his widowed mother was in less straitened circumstances than Lázaro's. Both mothers are of loose morals. The two pícaros' fathers are thieves.

Both protagonists begin their stories with a detailed account of their parents' comings and goings. Lázaro gives the sordid facts in an impersonal and somewhat cynical manner, whereas Guzmán pretends to relate all the shameful data as so many glories and distinctions. Lazarillo appears to be resigned and indifferent to his humble origin, but Guzmán is obviously trying to make light of that which rankles him deeply and has no remedy. His efforts to sublimate his shame and humor is pathetic to the thoughtful reader, rather than constituting evidence of depravity or cynicism, as has been asserted. It is pertinent to remember a remark made by Guzmán, referring to the story of his life: "And often-times, that moveth some to laughter, which indeed ought to draw teares from their eyes" (*Rogue,* II, 9).

Like Lázaro, Guzmán undergoes an initiation into the deceitfulness of the world immediately after leaving home; the former waif suffers a blow on the head, while the latter is sold bad food. A central theme in *Lazarillo* is that of hunger: about three quarters (i.e., Chapters 1-3) of the story are devoted to illustrating how the protagonist scrapes together enough sustenance to keep body and soul united. This preoccupation is uppermost in Guzmán's mind only in a few chapters at the beginning of Alemán's novel; thereafter the rogue sets his aim for a higher goal: that of accumulating a surplus, either for the purpose of satisfying his vices or of bettering his position in society. While Lazarillo will consider himself to have "attained the summit of all good fortune" with the position of town crier—in reality a notoriously base post—Guzmán strives after the fortunes to be amassed in business and usury. The disparity of ambitions would seem to reflect Alemán's desire to have his protagonist outdo Lazarillo in every way.

Lázaro and Guzmán both serve several masters. It is often averred that this procedure enables the authors to satirize systematically the representative classes of society. While it is true that Lazarillo's first three masters—the blind beggar, the avaricious priest, and the punctilious squire—are from the three estates of society (commons, clergy, and gentility), it does not follow that they are necessarily typical members of those classes. All three characters are individualized personages, not stereotypes. More significant is the fact that four of Lazarillo's eight masters are members of the clergy or of an allied occupation (e.g., the seller of indulgences); the archpriest for whom Lazarillo's wife works brings the number to five. Therefore it is apparent that the anonymous author concentrates his attention on specific areas of society, without attempting to give thorough treatment to all its levels. Neither does Mateo Alemán try to examine in detail all the components of the social spectrum. Indeed, the surprising thing is that in a novel over thirteen times the length of *Lazarillo de Tormes,* Guzmán serves only eight masters, the same number as his predecessor. Of these eight, at least three—the Italian Cardinal, the French Ambassador, the galley boatswain—can in no wise be considered representative members of Spanish society. The logical conclusion is that neither novelist is primarily interested in flagellating a typical cross section of society by having his protagonist serve the different occupations and professions. In fact, for long periods of time Guzmán works for no man; he occupies himself with stealing, begging, or managing his own businesses. Another point that has been forgotten is that the pícaro's contact with several masters can be interpreted not only as a device to satirize those classes he observes, but also to emphasize the miserable working conditions that he finds everywhere.

As outsiders living on the fringes of society, Lázaro and Guzmán take a dim view of honor, that quality which separates them from the accepted social classes. When he serves the squire, Lazarillo has ample opportunity to take notice of the pretentiousness and vanity of the gentility. Oddly enough, toward the end of the novel (Chapter 6) Lazarillo himself becomes preoccupied with appearances and buys upper-class clothes (albeit secondhand) and a sword, the symbol of gentility. However, he is not in the least worried about the real substance of honor, for he accepts the ignominy of a cuckolded husband in exchange for material advantage (Chapter 7). That is, Lázaro concerns himself only with external appearances, ignoring the virtue which is the essence of honor. Guzmán too prostitutes his second wife (II, iii, 5-6)—an obvious parallel with *Lazarillo.* The Sevillian picaro earlier dwells on the meaninglessness of the popular concept of honor, devoting most of three chapters (I, ii, 2-4) to an extended digression on the subject. He rejects the usual ideas about honor, finding that it is in reality the daughter of virtue. Only on the point of unfaithfulness does Guzmán agree with the common opinion: "mine owne Wife may take away mine honour from me (according to the opinion of *Spaine*)[19] by taking away first her owne . . ." (*Rogue,* I, 114).[20] It is interesting that Alemán later introduces (I, ii, 10) a figure similar to the squire of *Lazarillo* (i.e., a poor noble supported by his servant), but no reference is made to honor. Alemán expounds his convictions on this issue primarily in digressions.

The treatment of honor in *Lazarillo* and in *Guzmán* serves to illustrate the dissimilar narrative techniques employed in the two novels. The author of *Lazarillo* communicates his message largely by means of plot manipulation and irony. To express disapproval of the common ideal of honor, he introduces a character (the squire) who personifies much of what is ridiculous in this ideal. At no moment does the writer openly sermonize; the closest he comes to this is in the ironical remarks that Lázaro makes about his master. Even here, nevertheless, there is a marvelous semblance of objectivity, because Lázaro feels genuine affection, mixed with pity, for the squire. The latter is not condemned outright, although what he stands for is destroyed by satire. Alemán, on the other hand, often relies on the digression as a means of conveying his thought, rather than introducing additional plot material.

In sum, Mateo Alemán took *Lazarillo de Tormes* as a model for the structural elements of his picaresque novel. However, he rejected *Lazarillo*'s anticlerical ideology. In other words, Alemán borrowed the form, but not the content. He developed more extensively and convincingly the personality of his protagonist. Guzmán is more ambitious and complex than Lázaro, and engages in more important adventures. Several incidents in *Guzmán* are based on *Lazarillo,* but most are modified in form or spirit.

VI "The Rogue" *and* "The Watchtower on Human Life"

In Part II, i, 6 of *Guzmán,* the protagonist remarks that it is impossible to shake off the "Title of a badde name . . . The like hath befalne this my poore booke, which I have intitled with the name of . . . The Watch-Tower of mans life, they have put the nick-name of *Picaro* there upon, and now it is knowne by no other name" (*Rogue,* II, 56). The meaning of Guzmán's remark has been a topic of conjecture ever since. The usual explanation is that Alemán's memory failed him at this point, for the subtitle of "Watchtower on Human Life" figures only in Part II; the epithet of "The Rogue" would then be the invention of the publishers or the readers of the novel. Only the first part of this surmise is true, for the fact is that Alemán invented both subtitles. The preliminaries of the book make this clear. The approval of Fray Diego Dávila, given in January of 1598, calls the novel *Part I of the Rogue Guzmán de Alfarache.* The king's permission for publication, granted in February of the same year, substitutes the "Watchtower" subtitle. But the royal statement setting the price of the book, bearing the date of March, 1599, omits both epithets. Thus there are three slightly different designations for the novel. It is evident that Alemán was responsible for all, since the government authorities would be careful to repeat exactly the wording they saw on the manuscript.

Alemán's vacillation over the most appropriate appellation for his work reflects the basic duality of *Guzmán de Alfarache.* The first choice emphasizes the rogue's adventures, while the second calls attention to the book's doctrinal value. It is noteworthy that Alemán did not choose to emphasize the didactic importance of his novel when he submitted it to the ecclesiastical censor, Fray Diego Dávila. This detail disproves the theory that Alemán merely added the moralizations in order to make the picaresque escapades more palatable to the Church. The author's final choice does not unduly accentuate one aspect of his book at the expense of the other. The omission of epithets restores the balance between adventures and moralizations. Alemán upset this equilibrium in Part II of *Guzmán,* where he gave greater stress to the moralizing; the subtitle of "Watchtower" denotes the didactic emphasis. On the other hand, the reading public immediately perceived that the adventures were the predominant element in Part I, and consequently popularized the epithet of "The Rogue."

VII *Alemán's Affirmation of a Moral Purpose*

Alemán wrote two prologues to *Guzmán de Alfarache*; one addressed "To the Vulgar," the other "To the discreet Reader." Speaking to the latter, he affirms a moral intention: ". . . wherein my wit was wanting, the zeale which I had to profit others may supply that defect, by working so vertuous effects . . . For it was my sole purpose, to guide the prow for the publike good . . ." One of the criticisms he directs to the "Vulgar" is that they enjoy a story without considering its deeper significance: "Thou doest not make any stay upon the high moralities of diviner wits, but onely contentest thy selfe with that which the Dog said, and the Fox answered . . ." Alemán invites the discreet reader to collaborate with him in the moralistic interpretation of his book: "In this Discourse, thou maist moralize things, as they shall be offered unto thee; Thou hast a large margent left thee to doe it . . ."[21]

There is nothing unusual about Alemán's emphasis on the moral lesson to be learned from his work of entertainment. This was standard in Golden Age Spain, as well as in other European countries. As far back as the times of ancient Greece and Rome, an educational function had been assigned to creative writers by the preceptists Aristotle and Horace. The ideal of instructing while diverting had been dominant in the Middle Ages too, inspiring the exemplum and allegorical literature. Don Juan Manuel, Spain's first storyteller and a contemporary of Boccaccio, declares his intention of instructing and entertaining simultaneously in his collection entitled *El Conde Lucanor* (*Count Lucanor*). The Renaissance, on the other hand, valued literature for its beauty and generally did not insist on its educational function. The Counter-Reformation soon revived the concept of the double role of literature, turning to Aristotle and Horace as authorities.

After the Council of Trent (1545-1563), it was the usual thing for Spanish novelists to underscore the moral lessons to be derived from their writings. These educational merits were announced in titles, subtitles, dedications, prologues, and within the text itself; censors echoed this point in their imprimaturs. Uncommon indeed was the author who, like Lope de Vega, dared avow that his novels only pretended to amuse the reader (in this Lope imitated the Italian storyteller Matteo Bandello). This is not to say that from the middle of the sixteenth century on there was a sudden elevation in the moral tone of the Spanish novel. On the contrary, the novel and the short story were less inhibited than before; it is simply that authors began paying lip service to the precepts expounded by moralists. The most risqué novelists of the seventeenth century are often those who talk the loudest about the moral values of their works.[22]

Putting Mateo Alemán's avowal of a moralistic purpose into its historical context, it is apparent that he merely follows the custom of the day. Moreover, in his prologue the novelist gives equal emphasis to the lighter side of his tale: "That, which thou shalt finde lesse grave, or discomposed, presents it selfe in the person of a *Picaro,* or *Rogue*: which is the subject of this Booke." He persuades the reader to sport himself with these less serious elements, comparing them to "Pleasant and sweet wines, which must cheere the heart, and helpe digestion: and musicke for to please . . ."

General Considerations on Guzmán de Alfarache

The first line of *Guzmán* discloses that the narrator falls over himself in his hurry to commence relating adventures: "CVRIOUS READER, The desire which I had to recount my life unto thee, made me make great hast to ingulfe my selfe therein, without first preparing some things fit to be related, which . . . had been very needfull for the better informing of thy understanding: (for being essentiall to this Discourse) they would likewise have given thee no small content" (*Rogue,* I, 1). Alemán makes no further mention of a didactic purpose in Part I.

The continuation, on the contrary, fairly bristles with passages that declare Alemán's doctrinary intention: Guzmán's life is "onely to serve as a sentinell, to discover all sorts of Vices, and to draw treacle out of diverse poysons . . ." (prologue); "My purpose only was (as I told thee before) to benefit thee, and to teach thee the way, how thou mightest with a great deale of content and safety, passe thorow the gulph of that dangerous sea wherein thou saylest. The blowes I shall receive, thou the good counsells . . ." (II, 3); "Me thinks I heare him say, who is now reading, what I have written, that he will cast aside my booke . . . I confesse he hath a thousand reasons on his side . . . for, being truly (as they are) truths, which I treat; they are not so fit for . . . entertainment, as the understanding; being to be respected more, for the sense, than the conceit: These are not things fit for laughter . . . but are to be weighed with a great deale of study . . ." (II, 245). There are many more examples (see Moreno Báez, *Lección,* pp. 19-21).

It is obvious that the two parts differ greatly as far as moralistic intention is concerned. Part I announces such a purpose, but mostly as a matter of course; it concentrates principally on picaresque adventures. Part II does not neglect adventures, but focuses much more attention on the moral lesson. The increased preoccupation with ethics is partially due to the fact that Guzmán's repentance must occur in the second half of the novel. But even more important was Alemán's change of direction in his revision of Part II. The embittered misanthrope dwells long on the injustices of society—particularly those he has suffered —rather than replace the adventures plagiarized by Martí with similar ones.

VIII *The Ambiguous Morality of* Guzmán

The feature which more than any other separates the picaresque novel from other types of narratives is its artistic conjugation of the spirit of adventure with moral judgment.[23] The pranks that make up the material of the novel are usually immoral or reprehensible, but the author expresses a value judgment against the lack of ethics of these tricks; his end is achieved when the reader thoughtfully considers the contrast between adventure and moral judgment. The author of *Lazarillo de Tormes* fused the reprehensible and the moral judgment by means of irony (for example, in Chapter I Lázaro declares that his father "confessed and denied not" his thefts—an allusion to John I: 20). Alemán, in contrast, formulates the moral censure separately, putting it in the mouth of the mature and repentant Guzmán, who meditates on his past sins. The moral effect is obtained by Guzmán's reflections on the divergence between what he did and what he should have done. The juxtaposition of the ethical and the reprehensible creates a typically Baroque effect of light and shadow; this literary and psychological chiaroscuro is largely responsible for producing the aesthetic pleasure peculiar to the picaresque novel.

In spite of his immorality, Guzmán de Alfarache has a conscience. This is not due to a split personality, but to the fact that he is really two persons: the young rogue who commits sins and the mature man who relates them both as entertainment and as an example of bad conduct. This distinctive narrative technique of presenting the protagonist at two different stages of his development permits the picaresque author to achieve that most difficult of all tricks: to eat his cake and have it too. On the one hand, the roguish protagonist titillates the reader with unethical adventures; on the other, he rails against the immoralities he practiced years ago. The distinction between good and bad is always clear. Such is the method of this Baroque and paradoxical novel: underneath the unethical adventures flows the pure stream of Christian morality.

IX *Humor in* Guzmán

An aspect of *Guzmán* which has been particularly neglected by scholars is that of its humor. And yet it appears clear that the novel's wit was the main cause of its immediate and lasting success. The much greater popularity of Part I (sixteen editions in the first two years, versus five in a similar period for Part II) is to be attributed to the fact that it contained a larger proportion of humorous elements than the moralistic continuation. Alemán's contemporaries undoubtedly shared the view expressed by readers from the eighteenth century to the present: they much preferred the entertaining adventures to the somewhat tiresome moralizations.

Across the centuries the risible has been defined and classified in many different manners, but perhaps its most basic categories are verbal humor and physical humor. Verbal humor consists of amusing stories, jokes, puns, and the use of irony and satire. Physical humor takes the form of practical jokes and slapstick. Today, intellectual humor is considered superior to horseplay and is cultivated by writers almost to the exclusion of the other. This has not always been so; from the Greeks down through the seventeenth century verbal and physical humor were both extensively cultivated. Judged by today's standards, the wit of Mateo Alemán's time often seems coarse or crude. Contemporary storytellers found great hilarity in obscene tales and painful tricks; deformities and lunacy were considered laughable. Although Spanish writers customarily indulged less in bawdy themes than their peers in Italy and France, they were equally callous as far as human pain was concerned. In Spanish literature, as well as in the Italian and French, examples abound of how the public was delighted to see hair pulled out, sound teeth removed, faces cut, and worse. Cruelty was probably exaggerated in literary works, because everyone knew that no real suffering took place. People realized that in true life an elderly gentleman like Don Quixote could not possibly absorb all the drubbings that are administered to him in Cervantes' immortal novel.

The scatological afforded readers especial pleasure at this time. Two prime examples can be recalled in *Don Quixote*: on one occasion poor Sancho "vomits from both ends" after drinking a beverage apparently designed only for knights-errant (I, 17), and on another, he has a malodorous experience caused by extreme fear (I, 20). Another illustration is even more meaningful, because it occurs, not in an amusing novel, but in a scholarly treatise on literary theory. In the ninth epistle of his *Philosophía antigua poética* (*Ancient Poetic Philosophy*), published in 1596, Alonso López Pinciano discusses the risible in connection with the comedy. Like other Renaissance authors, he reproduces a series of jokes to exemplify different types of humor. Two of his principal specimens are true stories about persons who broke wind in public places. In one anecdote Pinciano soberly relates that an actor who accidentally committed this social breach on stage was showered with jewels by an elite audience of grandees and their spouses, so much did they enjoy the event.

In view of the cultural context, it is not surprising that Mateo Alemán, like Cervantes later, favored physical comedy over verbal when he wanted to make his readers laugh. One of the principal types of humor in *Guzmán* is the scatological. Among the many cases of vomiting and diarrhea that could be cited, the more spectacular are: Guzmán's ejection of the foul food served to him by a haggish inn hostess (I, i, 3); the abnormal intestinal discharge of one of Guzmán's mistresses, due to fright (I, ii, 6); and the smelly predicament brought upon the picaro by some "Hob-goblings" who buffet him in a blanket (I, iii, 1). Other instances of the use of filth for comic effect include: the "uncivill kind of fashion" in which two travelers less tolerant than Guzmán punish the hostess for her loathy fare (I, i, 4); the rogue's being caught with stolen eggs, all of which the apprehender breaks upon him (I, ii, 6); Guzmán's wild ride through mire-laden streets on the back of a boar (II, i, 5); and his accidental besmirching of his hands and mouth with ordure upon picking up what he thought was a pebble to throw at a dog (II, iii, 1). Several of these episodes resemble farce.

The picaro's clever deceptions constitute another of the principal sources of humor in *Guzmán*. The narrator takes great pleasure in relating his tricks: his duplication of the old folkloristic wile of stealing an object and selling it back to its owner (I, ii, 5); how he sold an Agnus Dei to a jeweller and then accused him of stealing it (I, ii, 10); his counterfeiting of sores in order to receive alms (I, iii, 5-6); his pilferage of whole barrels of conserves (I, iii, 7-9); his adroitness at discomfiting self-invited dinner guests (II, i, 3); the cheats he used to win at cards (II, ii, 3); his stratagem to swindle a merchant in Milan (II, ii, 5-6); how he cozened his relatives at Genoa (II, ii, 8)—to mention only a few of his deft frauds. One of the cleverest ruses in the entire novel is that used by Guzmán's parents to effect their first rendezvous (I, i, 2).

Guzmán is on the receiving end of some mirthful, if not always ingenious, deceptions: an innkeeper serves him mule meat, while abhorring the wickedness of the hostess who fed him bad eggs (I, i, 5); some catchpoles mistake Guzmán for a thief and give him a sound threshing (I, i, 7); streetwalkers repeatedly fleece the vainglorious rogue (I, ii, 8; II, iii, 1-2); and a kitchen boy throws a bucket of dirty water on him and then leisurely warns him to beware (I, iii, 3)—a common trick on the contemporary stage and apparently in real life. On occasion Guzmán makes veritable compendiums of the deceits practiced by the members of certain occupations. Particularly detailed are the descriptions of the knaveries commited by hostlers (I, ii, 1), cooks (I, ii, 5-6), beggars (I, iii, 2-5), and pages (I, iii, 7). Much laughter is derived from the statutes of an order of fools (II, iii, 1). Throughout the novel numerous interpolated anecdotes and jokes provide humor similar to that sought by public speakers who season their talks with light stories.

Alemán frequently uses language for humorous purposes. He takes particular delight in producing alliterations and puns. The initial rhymes can occasionally be preserved in translation ("[Necessity] is fierce, foule, fantasticke, furious, fastidious, faint, facile, feeble, false: onely she failes of being a *Franciscan*" [*Rogue*, I, 190]), but the wordplays are usually lost (for example, in II, iii, 5, Mabbe does not attempt to render the oft-used pun on *prima* ["treble on the guitar," "cousin,"] and *tercera* ["third on the guitar," "procuress"]).

Contrary to the practice of the author of *Lazarillo de Tormes*, Alemán makes little use of satire as a humorous device. In *Lazarillo* satire is the chief vehicle of humor, although there is also much physical comedy toward the beginning. The creator of the first picaresque novel employs the ostensibly naïve Lazarillo as a mouthpiece to deride the abuses and failings of the clergy, the nobility, and the third estate. In contrast, Alemán has his protagonist utilize satire only in treating his family background (I, i, 1-2, plus many subsequent ironic references to his "noble" relatives). After these initial chapters, with few exception, Guzmán narrates in explicit fashion, saying exactly what he means. One exception is the protagonist's ironic observations in Part II that he is aware that his readers do not need the benefit of his moralistic digressions (II, i, 1-2).

From the foregoing brief survey of humor in *Guzmán,* it is apparent that most of the more broadly comical elements occur in Part I. The original draft of the continuation was undoubtedly in the same burlesque vein, but in his revision Alemán replaced these passages, which had been plagiarized by Martí, with serious ones. Spanish humor thereby lost one of its best specimens.

X *The Digressions*

The digressions of *Guzmán* make up a significant portion of the total volume of the work. There are roughly forty digressions in each part, but those of the continuation tend to be longer than those of Part I. Whereas the moralizations constitute approximately thirteen percent of Part I, the percentage rises to twenty-three in Part II. A great range of issues is covered, from disquisitions on abstract metaphysical topics to down-to-earth diatribes against specific problems of Alemán's day. On the one hand, there are essays on the perfection of God's works (II, iii, 9) and the baseness of the human condition (II, iii, 2); on the other, there are philippics against gossips (I, ii, 5), the Genoese (I, iii, 5), deeds of invalidation (II, iii, 2), and annuities (II, iii, 4). Between these extremes are found discussions about honor (I, ii, 3-4), fear (I, iii, 8), humor (II, i, 2), old age (II, i, 3), rape (II, iii, 2), beggars (I, iii, 4-5), hypocrites (II, ii, 7), and students' landladies (II, iii, 4). Alemán has an inclination to repeat the same subjects, to treat a topic in two or even three different places. For example, he reiterates considerations on venal judges (I, i, 1; II, ii, 3), love (I, i, 2; II, iii, 5), charity (I, ii, 3; iii, 4, 6), gambling (I, ii, 5; iii, 9), deceit (I, i, 7; II, i, 3, 8), youth (II, i, 5; ii, 2), and bad wives (II, iii, 3, 9). In one case, the multiple treatments result in a contradiction: the author first claims that alms should be distributed only after the receiver is found worthy, but he subsequently declares that charity should be dispensed without question. Practical advice is abundant: the reader is cautioned not to spend on vanities (I, ii, 5), to treat his servants well (I, ii, 5; iii, 9), to be temperate in eating and drinking (I, ii, 7), and to make only short overnight visits (I, iii, 10).

Most readers probably agree with Guzmán when he remarks that some of his digressions are long and tedious (*Rogue*, I, 122), but the pertinence of his moralizing can not be denied. All the digressions evolve naturally from the adventures. With few exceptions (found at the beginning of Part II), Alemán's deviations do not produce the sensation of being space-fillers—as are those of his imitator Juan Martí, for example. No doubt the author's moral purpose could have been achieved more artistically by the use of ironic and satirical underscoring, such as that employed in *Lazarillo de Tormes* and *El Buscón.* The digressive technique deprives the reader of the pleasure of discovering for himself the writer's meaning. Its lack of subtlety and finesse suggests that it is aimed at a less cultured audience. But at the same time it must be recognized that Alemán's chosen method gives to *Guzmán* a moral scope not found in picaresque novels that are simply kaleidoscopic successions of adventures (*Gil Blas de Santillane* is a case in point). Despite its defects, the digression offers the advantage of permitting the author to make himself perfectly clear and to develop his case as fully as he desires. While not as aesthetic as an indirect narrative method, the digressive technique has been used extensively by such great novelists as Fielding, Hardy, and Tolstoi. It should be noted that in *Lazarillo de Tormes* there are short critical commentaries that can be considered the seeds of the long digressions in *Guzmán.*[24] Alemán greatly expands the relatively undeveloped satires of *Lazarillo,* turning them into extensive treatises, just as he amplifies considerably the narrative and geographical horizons of the first picaro.

That the moralizings are an integral part of *Guzmán* is demonstrated by Alemán's technique for introducing them. Only rarely are moralistic considerations read into the record of Guzmán's life by the facile method of reproducing sermons that he hears (this occurs twice toward the beginning of the novel: I, i, 1 and 4). Usually the digression serves either as a prologue to an adventure, thus building up interest, or it constitutes an epilogue—a commentary on the universal significance of the particular event. A good specimen of how moralizations create a sense of expectancy is furnished in I, iii, 1. Here the picaro alleges that "The Poore man is a kinde of money that is not currant; the subject of every idle Huswives chat; the off-scumme of the people; the dust of the street . . . the Rich mans Asse" (*Rogue,* I, 183-84). Guzmán believes that this is a permanent state of affairs and can not be helped. After these reflections, the reader fully expects that a mishap is awaiting Guzmán, and he is not mistaken. The rest of the chapter relates how the protagonist's uncle feigns to give him a home, only to terrorize him that night.

A moralization can add depth and meaning to an adventure when it appears at the end of a story. The digression goes beyond the action, distilling valid principles of conduct from it. Such are the meditations that conclude the relation of Guzmán's expulsion from the kind Roman Cardinal's home after he refused to correct his behavior: "For he that cannot be won with good workes, nor moved with faire and gentle words, it is pittie but he should smart for it and that rigour and chastisement should worke that upon him, which rewards and faire usage, were not able to effect" (I, 249).

Alemán often enlivens his digressions by inserting tales and fables. A typical example is that of the discourse on revenge (II, ii, 8), which is illustrated by two anecdotes and a story —the longest in *Guzmán,* excepting the four novelettes. The first anecdote tells of a lunatic who, having been bitten by a dog, drops a heavy stone on the animal's head when he spies him napping, remarking: "He does ill to sleep that hath an enemy" (II, 179). (This sketch is somewhat similar to one of the dog stories recounted by Cervantes in the prologue of Part II of *Don Quixote.*) The second tale emphasizes forgiveness. It is the pious legend of the Florentine Giovanni Gualberto, who forgave his brother's slayer and in turn was pardoned for his sins by the Christ of a crucifix in the church of San Miniato. The lengthy story, contrariwise, treats of sanguinary vengeance, in the style of the Italian *novella.* It relates the competition of two gallants for the hand of a beautiful and rich widow. One cavalier is favored and the other disdained. The latter has recourse to the treacherous subterfuge of spreading the rumor that he has spent two nights with the widow. The first gallant abandons his suit and becomes a friar. To avenge herself, the widow marries the defamer (although she refuses to consummate the marriage, supposedly because of a chastity vow) and cuts his throat one night when he is asleep. She then enters a convent.[25]

It must now be asked: Why does Alemán utilize so extensively the digressive technique? There is probably no single answer, but rather a number of contributing factors. Years ago, it was observed that the structure of *Guzmán* is much like that of a sermon[26]; this is particularly true of the digressions, the great majority of which could be preached from the pulpit. Like religious discourses, Alemán's dissertations consist largely of moral doctrine, with a liberal sprinkling of anecdotes to lend animation and interest. The similarity to sermons can in no wise be considered a coincidence; Alemán wished to produce the impression of being a strict and orthodox moralist. His novel was to furnish very tangible proof of his Catholicism.[27] For a person of known Jewish background who wanted to emigrate to America, this was very important. Therefore, although the writer was quite careful to make his moralizations germane to the action of his novel, doubtless in the back of his mind there lurked the realization that this was a method of overcoming his condition as a New Christian. Alemán's exposition of Christian doctrine in *Guzmán* may have been of help in his receiving permission in 1607 to go to Mexico.[28]

Other digressions—those that treat of friendship, wealth, honor—appear to reflect the desires of the have-not. It is known, through a letter recently brought to light,[29] that about the time Alemán was composing his novel, he was feeling lonely and deserted. Therefore it was natural that he should yearn for true friendship. Alemán's numerous commercial enterprises attest his eagerness for economic well-being. His deprecation of honor is a sour grapes attitude, typical of New Christians, toward those social values most esteemed by proud nobles.

A majority of the digressions of Part II represent an unbosoming of the writer's spite against his personal enemies. Through his novel Alemán takes revenge on those who misused him. Many of the references seem directed toward the persons responsible for his imprisonment in 1602: there are invectives against thieves, false witnesses, judges, and other law officials. Juan Martí is explicitly accused. The harangues against bad wives, usurious moneylenders, prison employees, and the holders of deeds of invalidation and annuities, are all transparent allusions to well documented episodes in the writer's life (see Section XI below on the autobiographical elements in *Guzmán*).

It has been suggested that some writers, Baudelaire and Dostoevski, for example, were inveterate moralizers because of a feeling of guilt in their own lives. Could this be another factor in Alemán's tendency to sermonize?[30] The hypothesis is attractive, for then the digressions, or some of them, would be a kind of veiled confession of a sinner who wished to ease his bothered conscience. The sermons would embody the writer's unfulfilled ideals. Unfortunately, there is little evidence to substantiate the theory. Alemán may have been guilty of losing money at cards, like Guzmán (he certainly displays a thorough knowledge of gambling), but there is no proof of this. The opposite tendency seems to dominate: the author of the moralizations takes a self-righteous stance—that of the infallible "Watchtower on Human Life" who searches out others' faults with his own virtuous light. A case that readily comes to mind is Guzmán's statement when describing the perversity of his first wife: "And I may truly confesse unto you, that in all that time that I lived with her, I cannot accuse my selfe, nor did shee ever tax me of any the least injury that I had done her . . ." (*Rogue*, II, 264). It is also significant that there are no digressions in *Guzmán* against lasciviousness—one mortal sin of which there is clear evidence of Alemán's guilt. The novelist treats the failing in Guzmán's adventures (I, ii, 8; II, i, 5-6; iii, 1, 7), but he does not moralize about it. Alemán, the sermonizer, accuses others of transgressing God's law, not himself.

In sum, the outstanding characteristic about the digressions in *Guzmán de Alfarache* is that they are intimately related to Mateo Alemán's personal life. Above all, they afford the novelist the opportunity to unburden himself against those persons who had wronged him.[31]

XI *Autobiographical Elements in* Guzmán

It has long been known that Mateo Alemán included many autobiographical details in *Guzmán,* especially in Part II.[32] The protagonist's embittered considerations on the impossibility of a man forcing a woman (II, iii, 2) may possibly reflect the threat of rape charges used to oblige Alemán to marry Catalina de Espinosa against his will. There can be no doubt that Guzmán's vitriolic diatribe against his first wife (II, iii, 3) echoes the writer's thoughts about his own spouse. Alemán's purchase of a lot in Madrid, on which he built a house and paid annuities, is echoed in the novel (II, iii, 2). After his marriage, Guzmán becomes a businessman and engages in unethical and usurious operations (II, iii, 2-3); as has been seen, Alemán was involved in similar dealings. Guzmán's digressions against the use of false deeds demonstrate the novelist's familiarity with these dishonest practices.

The rogue's studies at the University of Alcalá (II, iii, 4) parallel those of his creator. Furthermore, Guzmán returns to the University some time later (II, iii, 5) to take up a different calling—another coincidence with Alemán's biography. After falling on hard times in Madrid, the pícaro goes back to his native Seville and takes a house in the quarter of San Bartolomé (II, iii, 6), just as Alemán did a few years before finishing Part II of *Guzmán*. One of Guzmán's most damaging vices is his weakness for gambling (I, ii, 5, 9; iii, 9; II, ii, 3, iii, 5). Although no evidence exists of a similar propensity on the part of Mateo Alemán, his continual bad financial condition and his frequent use of gambling terms in the novel suggest the possibility. It is known that the writer indulged a passion for women—a frailty shared by his creature (I, ii, 8; II, i, 5; iii, 2, 7). Guzmán's embittered reflections on the difficulty of finding true friends (II, ii, 1) describe Alemán's situation at the time of writing.

All the examples enumerated thus far concern adventures or experiences common to the lives of Mateo Alemán and Guzmán de Alfarache. It is not at all unusual for a novelist to grant his own attributes or experiences to a character, even to one he dislikes. There are, furthermore, other details of a more intimate nature that reveal a close spiritual affinity between Alemán and his character. Such is the curious fact that Guzmán is of the same age as his author: this is made clear by an allusion to "a young King newly married" (*Rogue*, I, 106). The monarch is Philip II, who was wed in 1559; since Guzmán is twelve years old at this time, it is apparent that he was born in 1547, like Alemán. The common birth date led the novelist to forget the internal chronology of *Guzmán* and to make his character of his own age in II, ii, 1 (see Section XIII below).

Probably the most significant autobiographic trait that Alemán bestowed on his creature was that of being a New Christian (see Chapter 3 and Section II of Chapter 4). While it is likely that the writer gave this infamous ancestry to his protagonist in the hope that it would lend credence to his own claims of pure lineage, at the same time the device allowed Alemán to express covertly his sense of frustration at the interdictions that restrained recent converts from certain government posts, ecclesiastic prebends, religious orders, university degrees, and orders of knighthood. Guzmán's life, like that of all New Christians in Spain in the sixteenth and seventeenth centuries, is the narrative of an outsider struggling for social respectability. Like his forebear Lazarillo de Tormes, Guzmán aspires to having good clothes and a sword, the outward signs of honorable status. But Guzmán is not content with the modest position attained by his predecessor; instead, he yearns for true social acceptance, the kind that is achieved only by the affluent gentry. It is symptomatic that whenever the rogue accumulates a goodly fortune—by dishonest means, of course—he buys a handsome suit of clothes and adopts a new high-sounding name to support his pretensions to honor. In Almagro (I, ii, 9) and Genoa (II, ii, 6-7) he styles himself Don Juan de Guzmán, and in Milan (II, ii, 6), Don Juan Osorio. Like his picaresque character, Mateo Alemán tried very hard to accumulate wealth—his methods too were often reprehensible. He disavowed his tainted ancestry by claiming to be of an ancient Christian family (in his applications to go to Mexico) and by asserting that he descended from the Alemanes who emigrated to Seville from Germany (in his fake coat of arms). Guzmán and his creator, like so many recent converts, desired to migrate to America to escape from the oppression that they suffered in Spain; both were thwarted in their first attempts.

Perhaps the best example of the identification between Alemán and Guzmán is a passage that also proves that the former did not visit Italy. In II, ii, 2, Guzmán makes the remark that it would be a great wonder to see a pear tree bearing fruit at Christmas time. Then he hastens to add: "Of Castile [i.e., Spain] I say this, so that people from other countries which I do not know can not find fault with me." In other words, the narrator admits that he is acquainted only with Spain. Since Guzmán is in Florence at the time he says this, it is evident that the statement applies not to him, but to the author. In the hurried composition of his Part II, Alemán momentarily forgot to make a distinction between himself and his protagonist on a point in which they differed. The use of the first-person narrator in *Guzmán* inevitably leads to a certain confusion between author and character. In some parts of the novel the two are perfectly fused: for example, when the narrator complains how the public has changed the subtitle of his work from "Watchtower" to "Rogue" (II, i, 6), or when he makes references to the novel he is composing (II, i, 8; ii, 7; iii, 9).

The autobiographical elements in *Guzmán* noted thus far are presented in a straightforward manner; the experiences of the author take the same form in the novel as in real life, as though reflected in a mirror. There are other autobiographical experiences of Alemán which are related in a veiled style, much like that of an allegorical dream. Such is the theft of Guzmán's luggage by Sayavedra—a disguised method of portraying Juan Martí's plagiarism of Alemán's Part II of *Guzmán*. It appears likely that two other characters associated with the robbery—Alejandro Bentivoglio and Pompeyo—correspond to real-life persons connected with the pilfering of the true continuation (see Chapter 5, Sections V-VI below). The aversion with which the character Soto is drawn could mean that he too is the novelistic incarnation of a personal enemy of Alemán. Another hypothesis worthy of study is that Guzmán's odious mother may be in part an expression of a possible antipathy that the author felt toward his own mother.

In conclusion, it is apparent that Mateo Alemán included in his novel many autobiographical experiences. Some are treated in a conventional manner and others, allegorically. The predominance of these elements in Part II of the work is a consequence of: (1) the precipitation with which Alemán rewrote his continuation, and therefore used the material nearest at hand, and (2) the anger he felt toward those persons connected with the spurious Part II by Juan Martí. Had the Valencian not published his apocryphal *Guzmán,* Alemán's continuation would have been quite different; that is, more like Part I.

XII *The Pessimism of Mateo Alemán*

Mateo Alemán has traditionally been regarded as a pessimist, but only recently has this commonplace been put into its proper perspective.[33] Two types of pessimism need to be distinguished: *circumstantial,* which, as the name implies, has to do with circumstances in the short run, and *radical,* which concerns the essence of things throughout all time. Circumstantial pessimism implies that the world is evil, but that its salvation is found in Divine Grace. This doctrine is, paradoxically, an essentially optimistic view of the world, for although it regards the present as bad, it expresses confidence in the future. Radical pessimism, on the other hand, holds out no hope, because it judges the universe to be evil and absurd, with no hereafter. Radical pessimism is, then, entirely un-Christian. Since Mateo Alemán was a sincere Catholic who believed in the afterlife and exalted the perfection of all God's work, it is obvious that he was not a radical pessimist.

The passages of *Guzmán* which are usually cited as proof of Alemán's pessimism are the following:

All goes topsie-turvy; all Kim, Kam; all is tricks and devices . . . you shall not finde man with man; we all live in ambush, lying in wait one for another, as the Cat for the Mouse, or the Spider for the [snake. When the spider finds the snake off guard, she lowers herself by a thread and, seizing her by the neck,] holds her fast, never leaving her till shee hath kill'd her with her poyson. (*Rogue,* I, 128); This is the course of the world, it hath alwayes kept this track, it is no new thing, but even from the beginning . . . There is no helpe nor remedy for it; So we found it, and so we shall leave it; we must not look for a better time, nor thinke that it was otherwise heretofore. All whatsoever, either hath beene, is, or shall be, is still one and the selfesame thing. Our first Father was [treacherous]; our first Mother a Lyer . . . The first sonne . . . a thiefe and a *Fratricide* . . . (I, 185)

The first quote is a repetition of an age-old commonplace: that of cosmic strife.[34] The thought that constant discord exists among the elements and the creatures had been in the air at least since the time of Heraclitus (died around 480 B.C.), and was often repeated by Spanish authors before and after Alemán. The second quotation can be considered a restatement of the idea of cosmic strife, with Christian examples. The concept of discord among the creatures is here united to another common-place—that of the immutability of mankind. Since these passages are literary clichés, they are not necessarily to be regarded as proof of pessimism.

There are, however, other grounds for considering Alemán a circumstantial pessimist. An important piece of evidence is furnished by his repeated use of the emblem of the spider and the snake.[35] Alemán placed this device next to his portrait in the frontispiece of *Guzmán,* and referred to it in I, ii, 4 and II, i, 8. Beneath the picture appeared the Latin motto "Ab insidiis non est prudentia" ("There is no defense against an ambush"). The emblem seems to denote that the writer felt continually spied upon—a common experience for New Christians—and consequently that he distrusted his fellowman. However, as long as things went more or less smoothly, as in the years immediately preceding the publication of his novel, Alemán only alluded discreetly to his mistrust of mankind. There are no other signs of misanthropy in Part I. But under the pressure of the numerous acts of treachery that he suffered in 1599-1603, the novelist's pessimistic attitude toward man burst through the surface in Part II.

In the continuation of *Guzmán,* Alemán has his protagonist make such acrid observations as:

And therefore . . . it hath ever beene held one of the hardest and difficultest things in the world, to find out a true and faithfull friend.

(*Rogue,* II, 87); Amongst so many friends, as I had . . . I found very few, who had not an eye to the north-starre of their owne proper interest, and shap't their course by the Compasse of their owne private ends; having only a desire to deceive, not having any respect at all to the friendship they profest, being devoyde of all love, truth, and shame. (II, 88)

Certainly Alemán had good cause to be embittered. In addition to the nagging problem of his condition as a New Christian, he had just received several new thorns in his flesh: the proliferation of pirated editions of *Guzmán,* the plagiarism of his unfinished Part II, and the lawsuit that landed him in jail. All these misfortunes deprived him of income, besides the mental torment. It is therefore understandable that on taking up his pen to revise and complete Part II, Alemán should have taken a misanthropic view of the world.

In summary, Mateo Alemán is a pessimist insofar as he emphasizes man's deceit in Part II of *Guzmán* (in Part I his misanthropy is largely kept out of sight). However, he is not a radical pessimist, for he believes in the goodness of God's creation. In order not to exaggerate Alemán's pessimism, it is well to compare it with the thought of a great contemporary poet and churchman, Fray Luis de León: "Evil is not just a 'mode'; it is a profound characteristic of the cosmos, omnipresent and constant . . . there never was a time when evil did not exist. Man is ever the enemy of man; there was no golden age . . ."[36] This negativistic conception of the world is identical to Alemán's, yet it has occurred to no one to call Fray Luis a pessimist.

It is commonplace to contrast the "optimism" of *Lazarillo de Tormes* with the "pessimism" of *Guzmán.* The truth is, however, that the former novel ends on a note of hopelessness and cynicism, for Lázaro exchanges his personal dignity for material benefit. *Guzmán,* in contrast, terminates with the moral regeneration of the rogue. Lázaro is in danger of losing his soul, while Guzmán will save his. Since for a Golden Age Spaniard the salvation of his soul was the most important thing in life, it is apparent that the conclusion of *Guzmán* is far more optimistic than that of *Lazarillo.*

XIII *Time and Space in* Guzmán

Most novels are situated in an easily identifiable spatial and temporal setting. This was especially true of the novel in its earlier stages of development, when interest centered on the story, not on the manner in which it was told. In *Guzmán de Alfarache* time and space are described quite explicitly and in the plain terms usual in that epoch.

As for time, Guzmán never specifically mentions any date, but he makes numerous allusions to historical events, to his own age (as a child and youth only), and to the time elapsed since previous happenings. By combining these pieces of information, it is possible to calculate his year of birth—1547, the same as Alemán's—and his age at the time of certain crucial experiences. An approximate chronology of the picaro's life is as follows: Guzmán's parents marry when he is four. At age twelve he leaves home. The rogue goes to Italy when he is fourteen. He enters the service of the French Ambassador at age sixteen and leaves him four years later. Guzmán is probably twenty-one or twenty-two when he returns to Spain and marries; his wife dies six years later. When he enters the University of Alcalá, the picaro is likely around twenty-eight. Seven years later he marries Gracia. Guzmán is about thirty-six when he starts prostituting his wife. The rogue seems to be nearly forty when he is haled off to the galleys, and he is approximately that age when he begins to write his memoirs.

Each part of *Guzmán* covers a period of roughly twenty years. However, as with all human time, Guzmán's internal clock does not coincide with the duration measured by the rising and setting of the sun. Like all narrators, the picaro dwells for many pages on some short events and then glosses over several years in a single sentence. For instance, the relation of an ingenious theft that was consummated in a few days occupies two whole chapters (II, ii, 5-6), while seven years of study at Alcalá and a marriage are telescoped into a few pages (II, iii, 4). This compression of time is particularly evident toward the end of *Guzmán*.

According to the inner chronology of the novel, Guzmán commences work on his autobiography around the year 1587.

But in his hurried revision of Part II, Alemán inserted a passage —the description of Florence (II, ii, 1)—which was at great variance with the otherwise carefully conceived chronology of *Guzmán*. Here a character alludes in the year 1568 or thereabouts to a statue that was erected in 1594, and mentions that the present Great Duke of Tuscany is Ferdinand I de' Medici, whereas this prince really governed from 1587 to 1604. It is apparent that in his haste, the novelist forgot momentarily the internal time of his work and attributed to Guzmán his own age at the time of composition. According to the novel's chronology, the picaro is around twenty-one when he visits Florence, but Alemán makes him fifty-seven. The blunder was a natural one, since in Part I Alemán had given Guzmán his own birth date. This mistake is a good demonstration of just how closely the author identified himself with his creature in Part II of *Guzmán*. Similar inconsistencies are present in other Golden Age novels, the most famous example being *Don Quixote*.

The space through which Guzmán moves is represented just as lucidly as time is. The geography portrayed is concrete and specific, as was customary in the picaresque novel from *Lazarillo de Tormes* on. In accordance with Alemán's apparent purpose of outdoing *Lazarillo* in every possible way, Guzmán visits large portions of Spain and Italy in his wanderings, whereas Lázaro's travels are circumscribed to the area around Salamanca and Toledo. It is interesting that Alemán does not take advantage of the rogue's journeys to describe the countryside through which he passes. This lack of concern with nature is typical of the picaresque novel, and, it could be added, of Baroque literature, in comparison with that of the Renaissance. In *Guzmán* nature appears only on two occasions: as the settings for the rendezvous between the rogue's parents, and for the meeting of Guzmán and Gracia. In these descriptions Alemán associates luxuriant nature with carnal love—a recollection of the scene of man's First Fall in the Garden of Eden.

The reason for the absence of nature in *Guzmán* (except for the occasions just noted) is twofold. First of all, at this time nature was usually employed in novels as a backdrop for pastoral love affairs. Alemán did not deem it appropriate to include such material in a picaresque novel (he satirizes books of chivalry and pastoral novels in II, iii, 3), and he reserved his treatment of pure love for the interpolated novelette of *Ozmín and Daraja.* Secondly, Alemán is not interested in nature for its own sake; he concerns himself wholly with man. For the purpose of analyzing human passions and motives, descriptions of nature are superfluous. Significantly, there are in *Guzmán* many descriptions of cities—the urban geography in which people live.

CHAPTER 3

The Psychology of Guzmán

I *Introduction*

IN STUDYING the psychology of Guzmán, it is of the utmost importance to distinguish between two greatly different phases of the picaro's life: that which corresponds to the period of his roguish adventures—from the time he leaves home until he repents on the galley—and the much shorter period that extends from his conversion until the time he pens his autobiography.[1] In other words, there is a young, adventurous Guzmán—the "Picaro"—and a mature, repentant Guzmán—the "Watchtower on Human Life." The biography of the first Guzmán serves as an example of how not to live; the moralizations of the second, with whom the author identifies himself, hold up an example to be emulated. Many apparent contradictions in the rogue's personality are resolved by bearing in mind that the reflective narrator is a far different character from the protagonist of the adventures.

It is interesting that Guzmán shares only a few superficial characteristics with his predecessor Lazarillo: resourcefulness, cowardliness, thievishness, and a fondness for wine. The distinctive traits of Guzmán's personality are quite independent from those of Lázaro. There are four well-defined epochs in Guzmán de Alfarache's evolution as a character: childhood (I, i, 1-I, ii, 1), picaresque adolescence (I, ii, 2-I, iii, 10), picaresque adulthood (II, i, 1-II, iii, 8), and reformed adulthood (II, iii, 8-9, plus the moralistic portions of the entire novel). Guzmán's character development is heavily influenced by his environment, particularly by his family background. All the ambitions he nourishes, all the fears that oppress him, all his vices, are acquired at home as a child.

II *Family Background: Childhood*

Guzmán is born of an opprobrious family: his father is a Jewish usurer and thief (see Chapter 4, Section II below) and his mother is a prostitute, as was her own mother. He has a pampered childhood, without the correction of a father, in a home where moral laxity reigns supreme. Until Guzmán is nearly four, his mother carries on relations with his true father while living with an old gallant who has sired many illegitimate children with other paramours. At the elderly cavalier's death, Guzmán's parents marry, but the atmosphere of sensuality and materialism continues in the household. The usurer squanders the earnings that his wife had gained in prostitution and when he dies, the family finances are deteriorated. Although he is only twelve, Guzmán resolves to go to Italy in search of his paternal relatives. In order not to be known, he does not use his father's name.

Two characteristics stand out in the family background of the future picaro: the moral degeneracy and the Jewish ancestry. How do these social impediments affect Guzmán's psychology? The low ethical level of his home life is not immediately reflected in the boy's conduct, probably because of his age and his inexperience. This element will soon come to the fore, however. On the other hand, Guzmán's consciousness of his social inferiority as a New Christian affects his behavior from the outset. Even as a child Guzmán knows that his tainted pedigree precludes his admittance to respectable society and to important positions in religion, education, and government. It is no accident that the boy changes his surname upon going out into the world on his own—he knows that his father's cognomen would cause the doors to social status and power to slam shut in his face. (It is pertinent to recall that in Mateo Alemán's second application to go to Mexico, he exchanged his maternal surname of Enero—which smacked of Jewry—for the respectable cognomen of Ayala.) Furthermore, it is probably not coincidence that Guzmán plans to visit relatives who reside in Italy. From the end of the fifteenth century, thousands of Spanish New Christians fled to Italy to escape from the persecution that they suffered in their native country.[2] The boy's kinsmen were probably emigrants of this type. (It is appropriate to recall once again that Alemán's maternal ancestors were Jews from Italy.)

After concluding the narration of his family background and early childhood, Guzmán proceeds to describe his initial contacts with the outside world (I, i, 3-I, ii, 1). The emphasis in these descriptions is on his adventures, or misadventures, as he falls victim to society's trickery and malice. Having been indulged by his parents heretofore, Guzmán suffers a shock on learning that other people not only are indifferent to his personal welfare, but will try to deceive and exploit him. He readily adapts to the new circumstances, proving himself to be resourceful and able to swallow his pride. Although he has always been accustomed to giving orders, not receiving them, he serves an innkeeper for a short time. While at this job Guzmán observes that some boys of his age support themselves by begging. He decides to do likewise, abandoning all sense of honor. He begs his way to Madrid, and there becomes a picaro, living by his wits.

A peculiar stress continually recurs in the relation of Guzmán's transition from spoiled child to self-reliant rogue: an insistence on his piety. Guzmán gives prominence to the fact that, on the first day of his journey, he was careful not to eat meat, since it was Friday, and that he entered a church to pray when he felt distressed (I, i, 3). The following day he obeys a priest's exhortation to forgive his enemies (I, i, 4). Subsequently Guzmán emphasizes that he attended daily Mass (I, i, 6), and that he possessed the "light of faith" (I, i, 7). Even after becoming a picaro, Guzmán recounts that the first thing he did every morning was to hear Mass, and that he said his rosary and did other devotions daily (I, ii, 3). One sermon that Guzmán heard on the subject of charity and honor affected him so profoundly that he woke up that night and "made a repetition of the whole Sermon to my selfe . . ." (*Rogue,* I, 119). Guzmán takes such pains to stress his piety that it is obvious that he has cause to worry about what others think concerning his orthodoxy. The normal seventeenth century Spaniard took for granted that everyone knew that he was a Christian, and did not dwell on the topic. Guzmán, though a good Catholic, is aware that people will suspect him of heterodoxy because of his Jewish ancestry. Therefore, like his father, he makes a big display of his piety.

III *Picaresque Adolescence*

Guzmán's career as a picaro is a series of ups and downs; he seems bound to Fortune's wheel, for he is never long in one position. For a time Guzmán enjoys the carefree life of a rogue in Madrid. Then he works for a cook, believing that he can advance rapidly in the profession and soon retire comfortably. Guzmán is a model servant, doing not only his own duties, but also helping other domestics. All is not industry, however; as a picaro he had learned to gamble and now he indulges this weakness excessively. He begins to steal in order to have money with which to play. Since all around him are also thieves, he justifies his conduct to himself. On being fired by the cook, Guzmán tries to find a job elsewhere; failing, he returns to a roguish life. Presently he commits a large theft and plans to travel in style to Italy. However, his desires for fine clothes and loose women get the better of him and he squanders his ill-gotten wealth on fast living. With his usual resilience, Guzmán fits himself to the new situation and becomes the valet of an army friend, whom he serves faithfully and diligently. The soldier takes Guzmán to Italy, but there dismisses him because he fears his tricks. The picaro again takes up begging, learning the Italian refinements in deception. Guzmán still has some remnants of conscience, since he recognizes that by asking for alms he takes charity away from the truly needy. Paradoxically, the rogue's morality degenerates while he works in the palace of the virtuous Roman Cardinal. Here he becomes extraordinarily adept at stealing, takes up gambling again, and develops a sweet tooth—a craving acquired from his master. Guzmán becomes arrogant and ungrateful, not heeding the Cardinal's gentle reproofs. A redeeming quality is his liberality toward the other pages. In the house of the French Ambassador, Guzmán relishes playing the part of buffoon; being of a gregarious nature, he loves to have an audience before which to show off his cleverness and wit.

A pattern emerges in Guzmán's conduct as an adolescent picaro. His principal aims are social position and self-gratification. In spite of his elaborate praise of the freedom enjoyed by rogues, he prefers to serve in magnificent households. This inclination is not ethically oriented, but responds to his ambitions of rising in the social scale. To achieve this end, Guzmán cultivates his masters and also his peers. The rogue's social pretensions bring out, at times, his good traits: diligence, resourcefulness, trustworthiness, and friendliness. However, these positive qualities are marred by his shortcomings: Guzmán is too ambitious, greedy, lascivious, ungrateful, and addicted to gambling. He has degenerated appreciably in the few years since he left home, as if following his father's bad example. Still, Guzmán is not a reprobate. His crimes against society are misdemeanors, not felonies, and his ingenuity and prankishness make his behavior amusing. At this point in his life, Guzmán is simply a fun-loving juvenile delinquent.

IV *Picaresque Adulthood*

The protagonist of Part II of *Guzmán* is a greatly changed character. In spite of his social aspirations and his inferior race, the picaro of Part I is a happy-go-lucky type. The Guzmán that slowly comes into view in the continuation is far less carefree. He has deteriorated in the Ambassador's service from jester to pimp, and now has his own paramour. When circumstances force him to leave Rome, he determines to turn over a new leaf. This fresh approach to life is reflected in his magnanimous treatment of Pompeyo and Sayavedra. The resolution to live morally goes by the board, however, when Guzmán's purse starts pinching him. His subsequent thefts, carried out under an aristocratic guise, are much larger than any he has committed previously. Guzmán's motto now is: "Either to hang . . . or to have our dinners served in with Trumpets. . . . For a mans life is ended in a day; but poverty is a daily death" (*Rogue,* II, 127-28). His eminently successful swindles in Milan and Genoa enable him to return to Spain and to enter upon a business career. Guzmán's resources are such that he could live comfortably by operating a legitimate enterprise, but he seeks the fat profits to be had from usury. The picaro marries, apparently for money, but his wife ruins him economically and makes him miserable to boot. Oddly enough, the rogue does all in his power to pacify her. Finding himself poor again, Guzmán brazenly decides to find security in an ecclesiastical position. When the Church career is within his grasp, he falls violently in love and marries again. He is content to allow his wife's family to support him. When this situation comes to an end, Guzmán panders for his wife. This is the lowest point in his moral decline, which has worsened steadily for many years. Guzmán maintains appearances at all times, never openly confessing his dishonor. The sale of Gracia's favors restores the picaro's solvency for a time, but he dissipates the money and remains penniless when she leaves him. He then resorts to petty thefts, some of which are so abject that they recall those of Sayavedra. Guzmán is near the end of his career as a picaro.

Although Guzmán's autobiography takes up in Part II from the point where it left off in Part I, the picaro has aged beyond his years in the passage from adolescence to adulthood. There is an enormous difference between the youth who pilfers sweetmeats and the man who procures for his master. In the continuation even Guzmán's jests and escapades are often tinged with a note of bitterness. The mischievous rogue has become an individual with a tortured soul. The fundamentally religious Guzmán completely suppresses his qualms of conscience in order to win social prestige and power. As long as he has enough wealth to maintain the appearance of an aristocrat, or even of a respectable bourgeois, Guzmán leads a proper life. But when he is poor, the rogue will go to great lengths to gain money. That is, Guzmán's indomitable social ambitions cause him to sacrifice his religious ideals to materialistic desires. The defect of temporarily subordinating conscience to expediency is a most human one and is common in all times and places. However, in Guzmán's case the violation of moral principles is particularly dramatic because he is gambling with his very soul. As a Catholic, the picaro accepts the premise that he will be damned should he die in mortal sin. Guzmán's willingness to run the risk of damnation shows the intensity of his social aspirations. The picaro's gamble with his soul falls within a rich tradition in Spanish literature: that which culminates in the figure of Don Juan in *El Burlador de Sevilla* (*The Trickster of Seville* [1630]). Both Guzmán and Don Juan wager that they will not be surprised by death and will have time to repent after gratifying their temporal desires. Guzmán wins his bet, but the Trickster loses.

An equally intriguing recess of the pícaro's soul is illuminated by his attitude toward Sayavedra. Although Guzmán intensely hates his impersonator, he treats him exceedingly well. Guzmán's outward conduct is in the best Old Testament tradition, because it carries out to the letter the injunction that "If your enemy is hungry, give him bread to eat; / and if he is thirsty, give him water to drink; / for you will heap coals of fire on his head, / and the Lord will reward you" (Proverbs 25:21-22, Revised Standard Version). The Scriptural text is just as ambiguous as Guzmán's deportment: the metaphorical "coals of fire" have been variously construed as meaning "feelings of shame and remorse" or "God's judgments."[3] The latter interpretation, while prohibiting earthly retribution, in effect promises believers the most exquisite revenge of all, for it enables them to wish eternal punishment on their enemies. An invidious type of vengeance is thus fostered in the individual. Guzmán's devious generosity toward Sayavedra is clearly in accordance with the vindictive interpretation of the Biblical passage, because he does not forgive his enemy. Instead of truly pardoning Sayavedra and forgetting the wrong, Guzmán nurtures ill sentiment toward him and rejoices at his suicide. Guzmán's oblique magnanimity may reflect his Jewish background: it is noteworthy that the rabbinical theology of New Testament times did not take a clear stand on the subject "love thy enemy," as did Christian belief.[4]

V *Reformed Adulthood*

The last two chapters of the novel are the story of Guzmán's moral regeneration. (These chapters counterbalance the first two of Part I, which set the stage for the rogue's immorality.) The pícaro's reform is not instantaneous, but comes about gradually. He was never totally evil, not even in the period of his maximum debasement. For instance, when he deceived a saintly priest, pretending to be honest in spite of his poverty, Guzmán's heart was pierced with remorse on "considering the greatnesse of his sanctity and sincerity; and on the contrary, of my roguery and villanie . . ." (*Rogue,* II, 317). On being sentenced to the galleys, the rogue begins to meditate on the afterlife and asks himself: "What torment will they feele that are condemned for ever to a perpetuall paine?" (II, 333). Still, Guzmán backslides, relapsing into his old ways: en route to the galleys he goes along with the group in stealing a pig, and later purloins some jewels. On board ship he observes correct conduct and ingratiates himself with his masters. His reformed behavior is doubtless due in part to calculated plan, but there is also the element of sincere contrition. The picaro's final spiritual crisis and conversion are undeniably precipitated by his desperate situation on the galley; like so many sinners, Guzmán realizes that it is time to "get right with God." But this does not take away from the validity of his change of heart; many genuine reforms are brought about by a change in the individual's circumstances. Subsequent events put Guzmán's resolution to a severe test, but he is unshakeable in his virtue. He is truly long-suffering—almost martyr-like—when cruelly punished for crimes he did not commit. In contrast with his previous feelings toward Sayavedra, he really forgives Soto's offenses and tries to become reconciled with him. He meditates constantly on his sins and accepts his misfortune as God's way of bringing him to repentance. On the galley the rogue reaches his lowest point as far as bodily suffering is concerned, but spiritually he is at his apex. Guzmán has ceased to be a picaro, for he will voluntarily commit no wrong. He now begins to write his life story, hoping thereby to turn others from the path of vice.

The writer of the autobiography has repented from his mundane ambitions and is thoroughly disenchanted with the world's pleasures. Whereas before his reform his supreme ambition was to attain wealth and social status, Guzmán's present feeling is quite the contrary. Now he ridicules his past attempts to achieve these ephemeral goods, deeming them pernicious vanities and the cause of many social evils. He repeatedly attacks the cornerstone of society's privileged classes: the concept of honor. Guzmán finds that true honor consists in personal virtue.[5]

Although the mature ex-picaro has overcome his social ambitions, he has not been able to throw off the other primary characteristic of his youth: the awareness of his inferiority as the offspring of a Jewish convert and a prostitute. This is seen in the narrator's satirical treatment of his parents. In the two introductory chapters of Part I, which concern his family background, Guzmán speaks ironically, claiming to defend his parents' good name while broadcasting their infamy. After these initial chapters, he narrates in a straightforward manner, without ambiguities. This manner, reminiscent of *Lazarillo de Tormes,* sets this portion of the novel apart from the rest. Guzmán's reason for divorcing these chapters stylistically from the remainder of his autobiography is that their content pains him: he is deeply ashamed of the baseness of his family's conduct and ancestry. From a psychological point of view, the picaro must somehow sublimate or deprecate his profound mortification at his parents' disrepute: his method of pretending not to care is to take refuge in clownishness—a common compensation for a feeling of inferiority. The narrator who indulges in this pathetic type of mirth is trying to hide his true sentiments of shame. Another important factor in Guzmán's denunciation of his family's turpitude is that by divulging his inherited social disadvantages, the mature narrator rationalizes his failure in the world. He declares that the cards were stacked against him from birth. In one of the beginning paragraphs of Part I of the novel, Guzmán admits that ". . . I should goe about to cover mine owne weaknesses, by laying open those of my Ancestors" (*Rogue,* I, 2). If he were able, Guzmán would like to blame his troubles on his parents, saying that he inherited flaws of character and received a poor moral example from them. But he must avoid this idea because of the Church's position against determinism. However, in a deeper sense, Guzmán's parents are responsible for his plight because they passed on to him their bad reputation and Jewish ancestry.

Guzmán's outbursts against peasants (I, i, 5, 8) provide additional evidence of his New Christian psychology. Many recent converts inveighed against Spanish rustics because the latter were proud of the fact that they had no Hebrew blood in their veins.[6] While still a picaro (II, iii, 7), Guzmán had given a further indication of his background by wanting to emigrate to the Indies. Many New Christians (including Mateo Alemán) longed to go to America in order to escape from the oppression that they suffered in Spain.[7]

VI *Inconsistencies of Characterization*

Like other points of view employed in fiction, the autobiographical focus can use any one of several perspectives, each of which poses special problems. Sometimes the author makes the reader understand that the narrator is trustworthy (within the limitations inherent in any individual's restricted view of reality). At other times the writer makes it obvious that the reader should not accept everything that his protagonist says, and gives indications of what the facts really are. This is the situation when the novelist satirizes his protagonist, as in *Lazarillo de Tormes* and in the first two chapters of *Guzmán.* Between these extremes lies a twilight zone in which the reader finds it difficult, or impossible, to discern just how much credence he should grant to the narrator. This is particularly crucial in novels with possible flaws in characterization. When the narrator is an actor in his own story, it is hard to distinguish between those errors which the author deliberately makes him commit and those which are true faults in delineation of character. Such a problem exists in *Guzmán de Alfarache.*

Like any other narrator, the mature Guzmán does not give a perfectly objective account of his life. Since he is relating his autobiography with the major purpose of demonstrating the immorality of his past, it is reasonable to believe that he occasionally exaggerates his perversity in order to put his point across. But at the same time, he shows an inclination to defend his actions, rationalizing his shortcomings and attributing them to evil influences or to dire circumstances. Both of these tendencies are quite normal, for most persons are prone to overcolor or understate their good and bad qualities, depending on the end at hand. Therefore, many small inconsistencies in Guzmán's conduct can be attributed to his defective reporting.

In addition to these minor inconsistencies, which indeed may be intentional on Alemán's part, there appear to be some real contradictions in the characterization of Guzmán. In the second chapter of Part I, the narrator portrays himself as being unusually depraved when still a child. After Guzmán's father has died and his mother is too old to return to the occupation of prostitute, the twelve-year-old protagonist greatly laments not having a sister who could sell her favors and support the family. In following chapters, however, the author describes his character as being such an innocent creature that he could not possibly be this same precocious degenerate. This is particularly true in I, ii, 6, where Guzmán claims to be "as modest as any Maid" as far as the facts of life are concerned. Again, in Part II, iii, 3, Guzmán is cast in the role of a perfect husband with his first wife, who is a virago of the worst sort. But two chapters later he sells the favors of his beautiful wife Gracia, although he dearly loves her. Such erratic conduct is improbable even in the most unpredictable person. While many lesser inconsistencies can be attributed to the narrator who does not recall objectively all the events of his past life, these gross contradictions in behavior must be regarded as the author's errors in characterization.

Both of the artistic lapses just described are the result of the author's poor assimilation of source material. Guzmán's perverted wish for a sister is a parallel with the end of *Lazarillo*, where the protagonist cynically accepts his wife's prostitution as a means of livelihood. But after abandoning *Lazarillo* as a model, Alemán forgets his protagonist's premature lewdness (which is entirely credible in the light of his family background) and bestows on him the naïveté of a normal twelve-year-old. Guzmán's conduct with Gracia is likewise a duplication of *Lazarillo*, and illustrates Alemán's tendency to repeat himself and to follow sources too closely in his hasty revision of Part II. Guzmán's inexplicable patience with his first wife exemplifies another of Alemán's proclivities in the continuation: to insert autobiographical material with the purpose of taking revenge on his enemies. In Part II the novelist frequently reproduces situations from his own life and has his creature face them with the same attitude as he did (at least, as he saw himself). Guzmán's unhappy marriage and forbearance depict the author's experiences. On other occasions the picaro embodies the defects of Alemán's enemies—as when he is a usurer.[8] Thus Guzmán is a composite character in Part II, now incarnating his creator's virtues, now embodying the corruption of his adversaries. There is, consequently, an ebb and flow of virtue in Guzmán's life—a period of vice often follows one of morality, and vice versa. This effect of contrast seems to be a technique consciously employed by Alemán.

In spite of a few inconsistencies, the characterization of Guzmán de Alfarache is remarkably well done. The picaro's psychology is perhaps more complex than that presented in any previous Spanish work of fiction. Only the autobiographical "I" of the *Libro de buen amor* is as elusive and enigmatic as the protagonist of *Guzmán,* and this person certainly does not suffer recondite torments comparable to those that rack the rogue's soul. The complexity of both these characters stems in great measure from the fact that they are partially self-portraits of their creators. It will never be known just how much autobiographical material the Archpriest of Hita and Mateo Alemán included in their books, for they refuse to raise more than a corner of their masks. Herein lies much of the ambiguity—and consequently the artistry—of these masterpices. In Spanish literature, only the creators of Don Quixote and Don Juan achieved greater ambiguity of psychology.

CHAPTER 4

Part I of Guzmán de Alfarache

I *Mateo Alemán's Recent Convert Psychology*

FROM the very beginning of *Guzmán de Alfarache,* it is apparent that the author suffers from the persecution complex common to New Christians at this time. The dedication starts with the following declaration: "Of all those things in this world, which are wont amongst men to cause the greatest feare, I know not any that may bee greater, or of equall compare to that of an evill intention . . ." The novelist is so preoccupied with his calumniators that he devotes a special prologue to the "Vulgar," whom he identifies with his enemies. While it is true that many Golden Age authors prefaced their works with defiant remarks addressed to the ignorant masses, Alemán's words are unusually acrimonious. The reason for the writer's feeling of persecution is probably to be sought in his accusation that his enemies "are of obscure Bloud, humble Birth, and base mindes." It would appear that Alemán directs the charge of tainted ancestry against his adversaries in order to imply that his own lineage is not open to discussion. A later passage from *Guzmán* is illustrative of Alemán's mode of thinking. The protagonist is giving rhetorical examples of hypocrisy, and asks: "How often would my selfe fal a discoursing of other mens houses and their gentilitie, only of purpose to set my owne Pedigree a foot, and to shew that I was a Gentleman well descended? How often would I discover another mans defect, and find fault with it, and only to this end, that by taxing such a vice in another, I might be thought to be free from the same my selfe?" (*Rogue,* I, 213). Throughout the work, Alemán makes jokes about Jews (I, ii, 10; iii, 10; II, iii, 1, 5, 8), as though to reiterate that he is a Christian of ancient stock. However, Alemán was to reveal his true sentiments toward his people, belying this outward show of unconcern, when he made his protagonist—a self-portrait in many respects—a New Christian.

II *Guzmán's New Christian Background*

In the first two chapters of Part I of *Guzmán*, there are many subtle indications that the protagonist's father is a recently converted Jew. The picaro makes this disclosure in ironic fashion, for, like Lazarillo de Tormes, Guzmán begins the narration of his life with a mock defense of his disreputable parents. The rogue starts by alluding to the gossip that circulates about his father. Guzmán whets his reader's appetite by charging that his progenitor is a victim of slander. It turns out that the picaro's father was a Levantine. Modern scholars have not appreciated the importance of this term,[1] although in 1622 James Mabbe realized its significance when he noted in the margin of his translation that "*Levantisco* . . . is taken for an Vpstart, a Iew, or an Easterling, come from the *Levant*" (*Rogue*, I, 5). Although the word *levantisco* is susceptible of different interpretations, other data make it plain that it means "Jew" in this instance.

In the first place, Guzmán's progenitor, who is unnamed, settled in Genoa after departing from another country. Subsequent references in Chapters 1 and 2 make it quite possible that the unmentioned country was Spain, and that the Levantine was fleeing from the Inquisition. In Genoa this person became a usurer—the occupation most identified with Israelites at this time, as is well known. Not only for comic effects does Guzmán reveal that his father was pusillanimous ("Many times he himselfe heard that reproachfull word ["usurer"] as he past along the streets . . . yet he was of that good nature . . . that he tooke no notice of it . . ." [*Rogue*, I, 5]), for cowardice was one of the principal defects ascribed to Jews during the Golden Age.[2]

Continuing his sham defense of the family reputation, Guzmán divulges that his father was suspected of being a heretic, in spite of his obvious efforts to appear otherwise. The Levantine ostentatiously carried about a huge rosary with beads as large as hazel nuts, and was careful to be seen in church every morning. Still, people claimed that he held his hat in such a way that he did not see or hear the priest.[3] Another revelatory episode from the Levantine's variegated life is that he was captured by pirates and taken to Algiers, where he renounced his religion, became a Moslem, and married a wealthy Moor. Shortly thereafter he deserted his wife, taking all her money, and journeyed to Seville. In Spain he confessed his past errors, "reducing himselfe to the Faith of *Iesus Christ* . . ." (*Rogue,* I, 6). The fact that Guzmán's father changed his religion in Algiers means that he was not previously a Moslem; the phrase "reducing himselfe" suggests that he became a Christian for the first time in Seville. So it seems apparent that his original religion was Judaism.

Almost as damaging to one's reputation as the charge of heterodoxy is that of effeminacy. According to scandalmongers, Guzmán's father curled his hair and painted his face, making use of ointments and "slabber-sawces." The beauty of his teeth and hands was due to "the vertue of certaine Powders, Oxe-gals, Lees, Letherings, and other such sluttish and beastly confections . . ." (I, 12). The crowning glory of this unmanly splendor is a "fore-top" or tuft of hair over the forehead, with ringlets above the temples. Although at this time a substantial number of men engaged in similar womanish styles, effeminacy, like cowardice, was regarded as a peculiarly Jewish characteristic. Many Golden Age texts could be adduced; let it suffice to note that Alemán echoes this opinion in another passage (I, iii, 10). The foretop particularly was considered the mark of a Hebrew, as is shown by a quotation from Cervantes' *Los baños de Argel* (*The Bagnios of Algiers*): "Is not this fellow a Jew? / . . . His foretop shows it, / . . . a Jew wears [his hair] over his forehead . . ."[4]

Additional proof of Guzmán's Jewish ancestry is provided in I, iii, 1, where a Genoese calls him a *marrano*—the term applied to Israelites recently converted to Christianity. In II, iii, 2-3, Guzmán trafficks in merchandise and usury—occupations reserved for Jews, Moors, and Italians. Even in Part I the rogue has ambitions of becoming rich through commerce.

Guzmán's Jewish background did not escape the attention of Francisco de Quevedo, whose picaresque novel *El Buscón* borrows many elements from *Guzmán.*[5] In the second paragraph of *El Buscón,* the protagonist Pablos discloses that his mother was a New Christian. Pablos suffers from a feeling of inferiority arising from his family's bad reputation; an important factor in this inferiority is his mother's Jewish ancestry. It appears that Quevedo took inspiration from Alemán to make his character a convert and to make him ashamed of his disgraceful background. The mortification of Guzmán and Pablos at their parents' disreputableness undoubtedly influences their decision to leave home.

III *Guzmán's Mother*

If Guzmán's father is an opportunistic and unethical usurer of Jewish origin, his mother is equally unrecommendable. She is a prostitute, as was her mother before her. Guzmán describes her as "a lusty lively wench, yet grave enough withall; her carriage was very gracefull, and full of courtesie, her selfe young, beautifull, discreet, modest and of a well composed and settled behaviour" (*Rogue,* I, 14-15). The wench—whose name is Guzmán—and the Levantine fall in love at first sight, appropriately enough at the christening of an illegitimate child. Since she is the paramour of an old knight, the Levantine seeks the offices of a bawd to establish contact. Miss Guzmán is all too willing to oblige her attractive young wooer and invents a "witty device" to escape from the vigilance of her decrepit gallant. A trip is planned to Alfarache, a village outside Seville. On arriving in front of her suitor's house, Miss Guzmán begins to complain of a "sudden and grievous paine in her stomacke," and is taken inside and put to bed in the Levantine's chamber. The latter is hidden in a closet, and so the two fulfill their desires. This stratagem is a variation on a trick employed by two clever lovers in Lodovico Domenichi's *Facezie* (No. 331 in the selection by Giovanni Fabris, Rome: A. F. Formiggini, 1923). Alfarache, the setting of the seduction, is fittingly an Edenic garden abounding with fertility symbols: ". . . the fertilenesse and goodnesse of the soyle . . . which that river of *Guadalquiber,* makes the more famous, whose watry gullets purling along the banks, inrich and adorne al those gardens and fields that confine thereupon . . ." (*Rogue,* I, 17). Guzmán's parents enjoy other rendezvous.

After the death of her hoary knight, Miss Guzmán marries

the Levantine and they live happily for seven or eight years. The usurer dies after dissipating his wife's savings from prostitution. The family fortune is now irremediably impaired, for there is no daughter to carry on the tradition of supporting the household. The twelve-year-old Guzmán remarks wistfully: "Or if . . . it had beene my good hap to have had a Sister, to have serv'd a prop to my Mother, as a staffe to her old age, as a piller to our poverty . . . wee would have bid a figge in Fortunes teeth" (I, 28). If these thoughts seem advanced for a lad of his age, it must be remembered that Guzmán's mother has informed him completely about her way of life.

With the situation looking bleak at home, Guzmán decides to shift for himself and sets out for Genoa, where his paternal relatives live. There is no tender parting scene like that in *Lazarillo de Tormes* between the boy and his mother. In fact, Guzmán does not even say if he bade his mother good-bye. There seems to be an absolute lack of affection between them, although Guzmán notes that he was pampered at home. The picaro's mother reappears toward the end of the novel (II, iii, 6-8; see Chapter 6, Section VII below), where she is an avaricious and unfeeling procuress. (Like Alemán, Quevedo also reintroduces his protagonist's mother in a later chapter with the purpose of deriding her, and the satire is of an unusually virulent nature.) The ridicule of the mother is an uncommon literary phenomenon and deserves further commentary.

IV *The Mother in the Spanish Picaresque Novel*

The treatment accorded the mother in the picaresque novel is most unusual in Spanish literature. In Golden Age Spain, as elsewhere, the mother held a sacred position in society. She was the object of the utmost respect and veneration—perhaps due in part to an association of her with the *Virgen,* the mother of God. This popular awe was naturally reflected in Spain's literature. The esteem granted to the mother largely precluded her appearance in works of entertainment. The mother is virtually non-existent in the pastoral and sentimental novels.[6] She does appear, often unwed, in books of chivalry, but her primary role is that of spouse or paramour. The mother is generally, though not completely, omitted in the Golden Age theater; those dramatists who include mothers in their plays (Lope de Vega, Tirso de Molina, Guillén de Castro) usually emphasize their importance as wives or mistresses, and only incidentally allude to their roles as parents. It is inconceivable that a Golden Age drama should include in its list of characters a mother-figure such as Yocasta. This heritage of veneration for the mother still prevails today in Hispanic society, where the expression *tu madre* ("your mother") used in vain constitutes the most injurious of insults. In light of the foregoing, it is easy to appreciate the significance of the picaro's ironic or satirical presentation of his mother as a prostitute. Such an attitude is a contemptuous rejection of society's most revered institution.

V *Transition from Innocence to Knavery*

The crucial moment in Lazarillo de Tormes' life occurs when he leaves home in the employ of a blind beggar. On arriving at the outskirts of Salamanca, his master has Lazarillo draw close to a stone bull to hear a noise inside it; when he does so, the cruel mendicant strikes the boy's head against the bull. At this point the naïve child abruptly evolves into a picaro, for he realizes that he is alone in an inhospitable world and must use his wits to survive. Other picaresque novels include a similar experience which marks the initiation of the solitary child into the school of hard knocks.

Guzmán de Alfarache's first unpleasant contacts with society take the form of gustatory experiences. The day following his departure from home, the boy arrives in a famished state at an inn. The slovenly hostess sees that he is "a novice in the world," and treats him condescendingly, chucking him under the chin. Guzmán's reaction is of nausea: "O good God, how did her stinking breath annoy me! . . . if my Stomacke had beene full at that time . . . I should have spued out all within me . . ." (*Rogue*, I, 31-32). She has him sit on a lame bench and spreads a loathsome cloth with improvised bits of tableware salvaged from old crockery. The hostess then serves up some eggs ready to hatch. The half-starved Guzmán falls upon them "as a Hog upon his Akornes," but "felt the tender bones of those untimely

Chickens to crackle betweene my teeth, that they made my gummes to tickle againe. I must tell you truly, that me thought . . . this was but a course kinde of usage . . ." (I, 32). On realizing what he had eaten, the boy "fell a vomiting, till there was not any thing left within me. And even yet to this day, mee thinkes I heare those little chickens . . . cry still peepe, peepe, within my bowels" (I, 35). (It may be noted that the motif of the nearly hatched eggs was common in Italy and Spain; it is in Domenichi's *Facezie* [ed. cit., No. 297] and in Juan Timoneda's *Buen aviso* [*Good Warning*] II, 38.) Subsequently Guzmán learns that the hostess has been punished for her rascality. When she serves some of the same eggs to a couple of soldiers, they throw them in her face and rub them in her eyes, adding a handful of ashes for good measure.

Guzmán's second gastronomical misadventure occurs at supper the same day, when another innkeeper gives him mule flesh for veal. Although the culprit is haled off to jail, Guzmán can do nothing about the unpleasant sensation in his stomach. Three other mishaps follow hard upon the youngster's initial contacts with society: his cloak is stolen from him, he suffers a severe beating at the hands of law officers who mistake him for a thief, and he must pay a muleteer for transportation and lodging which he thought were free. At the end of Book I, Guzmán has formed a negative view of society, except for his acquaintance with two clerics, one of whom relates the story of *Ozmín and Daraja*. It is apparent that several of the first adventures of *Guzmán de Alfarache* have a bipartite structure, consisting of a rise—the seeming triumph of evil—and then a fall—its castigation.

VI *The Second Book*

If Book i is predominantly characterized by adventures, with few digressions, the beginning of Book ii reverses this emphasis. Chapters 2-4 are largely devoted to considerations about the concept of honor. Only in Chapter 5 does the novelistic action come to the fore again. As to the story, on the third day of his trip Guzmán serves two rich travelers, hoping to gain food and lodging, but they accept his aid without rewarding him. He would have gone hungry but for the kindness of a Franciscan friar. Later he works as a stableboy at an inn. His job entails helping his employer to fleece his patrons. Guzmán's first master, the innkeeper, belongs to one of the most satirized occupations in contemporary Spanish society. The major writers of the Golden Age liked to vent their wrath on the host who gave poor service and charged unreasonable prices.

Guzmán begs his way to Madrid, and being refused employment on account of his poor appearance, joins the ranks of the picaros, plying their typical trade of carrying baskets. Later he becomes the servant of a cook. He is diligent and conscientious in his work, but seeing the bad example of the other domestics, begins to steal. His largest theft is a silver cup, which he purloins from his employers and then sells back to them, after having it polished. This trick of selling an item to its owner is an old one in folklore, and appears in Timoneda's *Buen aviso* (II, 97).

Guzmán's thefts are trifling in comparison with those of his master the chef. While preparing a certain banquet, the cook pilfers a huge quantity of meat and fowl and has Guzmán convey it to his house. After going to bed, the rogue is awakened by some cats fighting in the vicinity of the booty. He runs downstairs naked to defend the spoil, and finds himself face to face with his mistress, likewise nude. Each takes the other for a phantom. The ensuing scene is one of the most comical in *Guzmán*:

> She schrict out so lowd on the one side, that the neighbours might heare her all over the streete, and mine was so shrill, that they might almost have bin heard all over the Towne. She fled as fast as she could drive to her Chamber . . . I strove to make as much hast to mine; the Cats they began to fly . . . upon the very first stayre as I was going up, I stumbled upon the Cat of the house . . . she scracht me by thee legges with her nayles: then did I verily thinke with my selfe, that some Ghost or other followed me at the heeles, and was come to carry mee away . . . (*Rogue,* I, 145)

The cook's wife was so terrified that her "retentive faculty had shrewdly fayled her . . ." and she covered the floor with ordure, which Guzmán had to clean up. He loses his position as a result of this embarrassment. Returning to his picaresque job of carrying, the rogue steals a large sum from a merchant and departs for Toledo.

In the Imperial City Guzmán is overcome by prurience, in spite of his youth, and has three unsuccessful love affairs within the space of a few days. He buys an elegant outfit, takes a servant, and promenades through the city, convinced that all the ladies are dying for him. The rogue finds one particularly to his liking and is granted a rendezvous for that night. He sends quantities of rich food for their supper. But just when their banquet is ready, the lady's "brother" comes home. Guzmán has to take refuge in a dirty earthen jar; there he spends the night while the lady and her lover eat the food and go to bed. The inexperienced pícaro has not yet learned his lesson. The next day the lady persuades him that she was not at fault, has him buy her an expensive gift, and gives him another assignation for that night. Guzmán arrives punctually, but the sly madame does not open the door. Later this inveigler and her companion are imprisoned for concubinage. The "duped-lover" story, like its opposite the "duped-husband" tale, was a favorite with the Italian novelists. Guzmán's misadventure is not exactly like that of any Italian story, but it is probably modeled after Gian Francesco Straparola's *Piacevoli Notti* (*Facetious Nights*) II, 5. Some details also appear to have been taken from Boccaccio, *Decameron* II, 5 and VII, 2.

Guzmán's second affair is carried on simultaneously with the first. Another female deceives Guzmán, offering him her favors in order to obtain expensive presents, but does not keep her promises. After his failure with ladies seemingly of society, but who in reality are streetwalkers, Guzmán tries his luck with a lower-class girl, a maid in a tavern in Malagón. They plan a meeting for the night, but a female donkey appears in place of the girl, and all Guzmán obtains for his efforts is a bloody nose. Shortly before, the lecherous adolescent had received a warning from Heaven: he fell when frolicking with the maid and almost impaled himself on his own dagger. After his repeated failures, Guzmán decides that the delights of love are forbidden to him and gives up. This chapter (I, ii, 8) is one of the liveliest and most entertaining in the entire novel.

In Almagro Guzmán joins a company of soldiers headed for Italy. Since he has money, he is accepted as a recruit in spite of his age. Several months elapse before the company embarks and during this time the picaro exhausts his resources. As a result, he loses his position and all his friends except his captain. The rogue shows his gratitude by becoming his commander's servant. The captain is poor, so Guzmán provides for his needs by stealing (just as Lazarillo did for the punctilious squire). One of the picaro's clever thefts involves selling a piece of jewelry to an Israelite usurer, and then making it appear that the latter had robbed him. The captain begins to mistrust Guzmán because of his adeptness at larceny and once they arrive in Italy, discharges the rogue.

VII *The Third Book*

Book iii is devoted almost entirely to adventures, with few digressions. Guzmán arrives in Genoa and tries to establish contact with his father's family. He is mistreated by all in this commercial city: "There was not that man to whom I made my selfe knowne, that did not releeve me with a box on the eare . . . and he that did least hurt or disgrace me, did not stick to spit in my face . . ." (*Rogue,* I, 186). Later Guzmán says of Genoese businessmen that they "carrie their consciences in torne pockets . . . whereby they quickly come to be lost, and scarce one amongst them all . . . hath a good and sound conscience" (I, 209). This negative opinion of the Genoese is a faithful reflection of the seventeenth century Spanish attitude toward the inhabitants of the Ligurian republic. To the Golden Age Spaniard, the thriving city of Genoa represented an unscrupulous materialism that conflicted with the Spanish ideal of honor and nobility.[7] This national prejudice stemmed from the fact that most of Spain's economy was in the hands of Genoese usurers. It is also possible that Alemán felt a special antipathy toward Genoa as the result of a private experience: in 1568 he had had recourse to a loan from Esteban Grillo, a Genoese moneylender.[8] In passing, it may be noted that Guzmán's father was all the more despicable in the eyes of the contemporary Spanish reader because of his Genoese citizenship.

Searching for his relatives, Guzmán meets an uncle and is invited to his home. Late that night the picaro is awakened and tossed in a blanket by some servants dressed as devils; he is so terror-stricken that he ends up covered with his own filth. It will be remembered that in *Don Quixote* (I, 17), Sancho Panza also falls victim of a blanket-tossing—a typically Spanish prank.

Chapters 2-6 treat at length a problem current in Europe since the thirteenth century: that of the "false beggar"—the able-bodied vagrant who preferred to live from public charity rather than earn a living. The able-bodied mendicant was a social problem in France, Italy, and Spain from the Middle Ages, and the type passed into the literature of these countries at an early date.[9] To awaken pity in almsgivers, the false beggars carried canes or crutches, simulated wounds, captured children and disfigured them. They organized bands, often in collaboration with thieves. There were several aggravating factors peculiar to Spain: the "Old Christians" who refused to work; the opportunity of acquiring a fortune in the New World without real labor, which led to a feeling of "Why work?"; the possibility of enlisting as a mercenary in an army, which induced sloth; the attitude of the Church, which fomented mendicity by its indiscriminate distribution of alms.

Although it has often been held that the Spanish picaresque novel arose from social and economic conditions of the sixteenth and seventeenth centuries, in fact these conditions were present long before they were given literary treatment. The sociological and economic aspects of the picaresque novel have been overemphasized by some critics, to the detriment of its appreciation as literature. The simple truth is that the same conditions had prevailed for several hundred years in Spain, as well as in France and Italy, without producing the picaresque novel. The principal explanation for the birth of this genre must be sought in the artistic genius of the anonymous author of *Lazarillo de Tormes* and of Mateo Alemán, not in the social circumstances prevalent at the time they wrote.

Most literary treatments of the false-beggar motif had a double purpose: to entertain, exploiting the comic qualities of the tricks played by this antisocial type, and at the same time, to warn readers about his exploitation of the public's kindheartedness in order to live without toiling. The most extensive exposition of the motif in Spanish literature is in *Guzmán de Alfarache*.

After hurriedly leaving Genoa, Guzmán goes to Rome, where he receives instruction in the art of begging. He joins a fraternity of mendicants who have set up ordinances to govern their activities, with a view to insuring their success and of preserving good relations with the public. The head of this brotherhood is Micer Morcón, "the Prince of Roguery, and the Arch-begger of Christendome" (*Rogue,* I, 197). Guzmán exposes many secrets and ruses of the Italian beggars, who surpassed paupers of other nations in refinements and cruelty. The rogue learns how to provoke compassion in almsgivers with sham sores. A merciful Cardinal takes Guzmán home and calls two doctors to cure him. They discover that his canker is self-inflicted, but exploit the Cardinal, drawing out the "treatment" over a long period. After he is pronounced well, Guzmán becomes a page in the prelate's service.

Chapter 7 begins with a long digression on the transitoriness of earthly things, but then concentrates on adventures. Guzmán boasts of the skill he displayed in purloining preserves from his master the Cardinal. The picaro extracts the sweetmeats from their depository by lifting the lid with a wedge and stick. One day his arm becomes stuck in the trunk and the church dignitary discovers him. It is evident that this episode is based on Chapter 2 of *Lazarillo de Tormes,* where Lázaro steals bread from the trunk of the priest of Maqueda. Although the basic situation is identical, the circumstances are quite different. Lazarillo's master is a penurious and cruel cleric who nearly starves his boy to death. In contrast, the Cardinal is not only Guzmán's kindest master, but is the most moral character in the entire novel. The rogue is not forced by hunger to steal, like Lazarillo, but does so merely to satisfy a craving for sweets. Guzmán receives a mild punishment from his master, whereas Lázaro is knocked unconscious. In reworking his model, Alemán manifests his religious orthodoxy by transforming the bitterest anticlerical episode in *Lazarillo,* converting the materialistic and brutal cleric of Maqueda into a benevolent and gentle prelate.

Chapters 8-10 consist largely of practical jokes. Guzmán exhibits his wit by stealing his indulgent master's preserves, giving "hotfeet" to his companions, cozening sellers of sweetmeats, and throwing dirty water on streetwalkers. However, the rogue falls prey to the vice of gambling, and this causes his dismissal. After living off friends for a time, he becomes the buffoon of the French Ambassador in Rome. In the latter's house he listens to the story of *Dorido and Clorinia,* which closes Part I.

CHAPTER 5

Part II of Guzmán: *Response to the Apocryphal Continuation*

I *Juan Martí's Continuation*

TO APPRECIATE more fully Part II of Mateo Alemán's *Guzmán de Alfarache*, it is necessary to consider the spurious continuation published in Valencia in August of 1602, under the pseudonym of "Mateo Luján de Sayavedra." It is probable that the author would have remained forever anonymous, had not Alemán unmasked him. In the authentic Part II, a character reveals that the unscrupulous imitator is a Valencian lawyer named Juan Martí. It is interesting that Alemán disclosed the identity of his literary antagonist only through his characters. In the prologue of his second part he refrained from naming Martí, divulging only that the unknown author was a native of Valencia and that he plagiarized his manuscript and plans for the continuation of his novel.

Alemán further claims in the prologue that he had finished his Part II and that Martí stole all his ideas. This statement agrees with a declaration that the picaresque novelist had made in the preliminaries of Part I, where he affirmed that his continuation was already completed. However, there is strong evidence to disprove the assertion. First of all, in the dedication of his Part II, Alemán contradicts his other allegations, stating that Martí "aborted the embryo" of the authentic continuation. The term "embryo" clearly implies that the manuscript was incomplete. Secondly, in the prologue to his Part II, Alemán points out many glaring defects in the Valencian's novel; had Martí's work been a plagiarism it would not have contained these errors. As a matter of fact, it is possible to estimate the extent of the

Valencian's theft. Like Alemán, Martí divides his work into three Books, each of eight to eleven chapters. Book i and Chapters 1-3 of Book ii—about a third of the total volume—are readable, though marred by serious flaws of technique. Thereafter the action declines rapidly and the novel degenerates into a series of pedantic and boring digressions. The abrupt change in quality makes it plain that Martí's plagiarisms are largely, if not entirely, restricted to the first third of his novel. Therefore it is apparent that Martí could not have based his *Guzmán* on a finished manuscript. Moreover, by no means all of the section containing the plagiarisms is based on Alemán's original; large portions of the first chapters bear the stamp of Martí's work. The logical conclusion is that the Valencian read or heard about Alemán's incomplete Part II, but did not have the opportunity to copy from the manuscript. In any case, Martí's thefts caused Alemán to rewrite most (but probably not all) of the original draft of the continuation.

II *Alemán's Criticism of the Spurious* Guzmán

In his prologue to the reader of Part II, Alemán comments extensively on Martí's work. He first professes admiration for the latter's "great learning, his nimble wit, his deepe judgement; his pleasant conceits, and his generall knowledge in all humane and divine letters . . ." and claims that he would be proud to have penned such polished digressions. These affirmations are probably ironic. The creator of Guzmán then proceeds to consider the faults of the spurious continuation. Alemán compares Martí's novel to a woman whose features are ideal when contemplated separately but whose beauty fails through lack of harmony. He criticizes the Valencian for insufficient study of Part I of *Guzmán*. Martí's hero is a mediocre student, whereas Alemán had given him a careful preparation for the priesthood. The Valencian has missed the whole point, according to Alemán, for the latter's purpose was to create the perfect man, after following his painful peregrinations along the road of vice. (It should be noted that this purpose was only implicit in Part I, in the moral uprightness of the narrator; Alemán had not previously announced openly the intention of producing a faultless creature.) Furthermore, Martí's protagonist is not a great thief, as he was supposed to be, but a cheap cape-snatcher. The false Guzmán does not take revenge on his Genoese relatives, as promised in Part I (iii, 1), and leaves other episodes unfinished. Also, the Valencian makes the mistake of introducing real persons into his work of fiction, including their true names. Alemán concludes that it is impossible for one writer to compose an artistic continuation of another's work, because he can not penetrate the original plans for character and plot development; Martí's novel was consequently predestined to be far inferior to his own. Though not benevolent, Alemán is relatively mild in his criticism of the apocryphal *Guzmán,* but only because he is reserving his true vengeance for a later moment. Starting in Part II, i, 7, Alemán was to unleash a violent allegorical satire against Martí and his spurious continuation.

III *Alemán's Part II: Padding*

Part II of *Guzmán* starts very slowly. The first four chapters consist almost entirely of digressions and anecdotes. In Chapter 1 there is no action; as the subtitle indicates, Guzmán simply "excuseth the processe of his discourse, craveth attention, gives notice of his intent . . ." (*Rogue,* II, 1). Included are a couple of tales, one concerning a lunatic that throws stones, and another about a stingy man who makes his wife eat some withered radishes. Chapter 2 is likewise devoid of adventures; Guzmán reveals that he served the French Ambassador as a go-between, and digresses on several topics. Almost half the space is given over to five anecdotes: two comedians conclude that jokes can not be prepared beforehand; two liars exaggerate the size of the antlers on deer they have killed; a buffoon refuses to divulge the name of a prince's critic, saying that the latter is a member of the Holy Trinity; a town crier claims to find a lost ass when he discovers a youth who says he has never been in love; and a nun asserts that all her gallant's accomplishments are due to her inspiration.

Chapter 3 is largely devoted to a digression on several kinds of deceits, which are illustrated by three tales: a student tricks a beggar into leaving home for a night and steals his hens; the same student loses the chickens to some college companions who pretend to be officers of the law; and a needy poet shames a rich prince into aiding him by praising and rewarding him for a poem. Alemán's considerations on deceit lead him by devious paths to reflect on old age; this subject is adorned by a lengthy fable (found in Jaime Juan Falcón's *Operum poeticorum*, libri V, Madrid, 1600): several animals ask Jupiter to shorten their lives so they may suffer less, and these years are added to man's original life span of thirty years; however, man must endure sufferings similar to those of the animals. Toward the end of the chapter, the rogue finally appears on stage as an actor, rather than a raconteur, and plays a prank on an importunate soldier and scholar who force themselves upon the French Ambassador at dinnertime. To pacify them, another dinner guest relates the novelette of *Don Luis de Castro;* this occupies Chapter 4.

It is apparent from this summary that Martí's continuation adversely affected Alemán's, forcing him to deviate from his original plans. The lack of action in the initial chapters of Part II and the recourse to folkloristic material for padding, clearly indicate that this section was hastily written by Alemán. In Part I of *Guzmán* (twenty-eight chapters in all) he had included only seventeen tales; in the first three chapters alone of Part II, he introduced eleven. No other part of the novel suffers from such a dearth of action. The interpolation of a novelette toward the beginning of the continuation is additional evidence of a hurried revision, for Alemán normally places his novelettes at the end of a Book, as a change from numerous preceding picaresque episodes. The fact that both novelettes of Part II are based on easily recognizable models, rather than being highly elaborated stories like those of Part I, is added proof that Alemán composed his continuation under pressure and, in order to save time, relied heavily on literary sources.

An explanation must be sought for Alemán's deviation from his usual procedure of starting each Book with a strong entrée of action, for Guzmán's adventures really start in Chapter 5. Above, it was seen that Book i of Martí's Part II undoubtedly contains many episodes imitated from Alemán's original continuation. These plagiarisms came from the beginning of Alemán's manuscript, because they take up Guzmán's story where it left off at the end of Part I. The creator of Guzmán omitted this beginning section—probably his Book i, consisting of seven or eight chapters—because it was plagiarized by Martí. He then hurriedly penned the three digressive chapters to replace them. This explains why the novelette (which normally would have come at the conclusion of the Book) is interpolated in Chapter 4. Alemán perhaps found it quicker to bring together a number of anecdotes, of which he had an immense repertory, rather than to write a connected series of adventures to replace the stolen ones.

IV *Adventures*

Chapters 5 and 6 afford a vivid contrast to the languor of the first pages of Part II. These chapters are similiar to I, ii, 8, in that they treat of unsuccessful amours, are of Italian inspiration, and are among the most entertaining in the novel. A Roman matron offers to see Guzmán (concerning an interview with his master), but with the purpose of punishing him for offending her chastity. The rogue is first kept waiting for several nights, and when finally admitted into the house, is thrust into an inclosure where night pots are emptied. This episode appears to be an original reelaboration of the *Decameron* II, 5 (where Andreuccio is left one night in a similar malodorous nook), and VIII, 7 (where an enamoured scholar spends a fruitless night in the snow, waiting for his sweetheart to open the door); also, Alemán doubtless knew Ser Giovanni's treatment of the same general situation (*Pecorone* II, 2).

As in I, ii, 8, Alemán exploits the humorous possibilities of filth in these chapters. Guzmán not only passes a stenchful night, but a few days later involuntarily rides a pig through impure streets, ending up covered from head to toe with slime. While these chastisements are immensely comical, they are so emphatic as to appear Heaven-sent. The picaro's customary bad luck is evident in the fact that he bears the punishment deserved by his master, for Guzmán is only an agent of the latter.

It is possible that Chapters 5 and 6 are from Alemán's original draft of Part II, although the master for whom Guzmán procured was not necessarily the Ambassador. In ii, 2 of Martí's continuation, Guzmán is also a go-between for his master; the Valencian could have been inspired in a general way by Alemán's version, but did not imitate it closely because of its predominantly scatological nature. Martí grafted the pandering episode upon another taken from Part I of *Guzmán*: that of the pilfering cook and his alcoholic wife.

As a consequence of his misadventure with the hog, Guzmán is whistled at and mocked by all the street urchins of Rome. This circumstance sets the stage for the entrance (in Chapter 7) of a young man, Sayavedra, who saves Guzmán from an unruly mob, but refuses to identify himself. He persuades Guzmán to take a trip throughout Italy. Guzmán plans to visit in Siena a friend named Pompeyo, whom he has never seen. Sayavedra impersonates Guzmán and receives his baggage from Pompeyo; then the impostor and his accomplices flee.

V *Pompeyo*

Book ii has to do with Guzmán's subsequent relations with Sayavedra. But before turning the spotlight on the two rogues, Alemán concludes Guzmán's strange friendship with Pompeyo. It has been noted[1] that this character is poorly tied in with the main action. Guzmán emphasizes that, although they had never met, he and Pompeyo were very good friends and had corresponded. Since Pompeyo does not appear elsewhere in the novel, the question naturally arises as to how the two became fast friends, because they are not related and have no business connections. Pompeyo's only justification for appearing in the novel is that he unintentionally turns Guzmán's luggage over to Sayavedra. To accomplish such a modest task it was not necessary to introduce an individualized character—any innkeeper or casual friend would have sufficed. Pompeyo's role is clearly not for novelistic purposes.

It seems likely that Alemán inserted this mysterious personage for allegorical reasons. A large part of Alemán's continuation is autobiographical, with Guzmán suffering the same injustices and tribulations as his creator had undergone during the years immediately preceding the writing of Part II of *Guzmán*. At times

Alemán subjects his character to experiences identical to his own (debts, imprisonment, marriage to an incompatible wife, involvement with unscrupulous businessmen); at other times he allegorizes painful encounters. Such is his treatment of Martí's unethical continuation of *Guzmán de Alfarache.* The entire second book of Alemán's Part II is a veiled denunciation of the Valencian author and his apocryphal protagonist, Sayavedra. The allegory is quite simple: Martí's plagiarism is represented by the theft of Guzmán's luggage by Sayavedra. It also seems likely that Alemán alludes to other persons connected with the publication of Martí's work.

As already noted, Pompeyo's only function in *Guzmán* is inadvertently to turn Guzmán's belongings over to the impostor Sayavedra. This is, in allegorical terms, much the same role as that played by the printer of the spurious *Guzmán,* who, by issuing the book, handed Alemán's property over to Martí. The publisher of the apocryphal *Guzmán* was a Valencian called Pedro Patricio Mey; it will be noticed that the somewhat unusual name Pompeyo is an anagram of P[edr]o P[atrici]o Mey.[2] While it is unsound to base conclusions on anagrams, this shred of evidence does fit in with the oblique scheme Alemán uses to pulverize his literary enemy in the continuation of *Guzmán.* That Alemán was thinking in terms of anagrams while treating the apocryphal continuation is evident in his explanation of how Martí chose the pseudonym "Mateo Luján" (II, ii, 4; see Section VII below).

VI *Alejandro Bentivoglio*

In Chapter 1 of Book ii, Guzmán sees that Pompeyo is tired of his company and decides to journey to Florence. On leaving Siena he encounters Sayavedra, who begs his forgiveness and enters his service. After admiring the beauties of Florence, the rogues travel to Bologna, where they meet Alejandro Bentivoglio, an accomplice in the theft of Guzmán's luggage. The pícaro takes Bentivoglio to court, but the latter's rich and influential father has a venal judge imprison Guzmán for defamation, although it is public knowledge that Alejandro stole the goods.

Guzmán's indignation at this injustice is so heartfelt that Alemán appears to be expressing his own rage toward a similar miscarriage of justice committed against himself. He exclaims:

There is no sword that hath so sharpe and keene an edge, as Calumnie, and false Accusation . . . My businesse was plaine . . . there was not a man, neither within, nor without the Towne, that did not know, all was true, that I had delivered; and all this did plainly appeare to the Iudge to be so . . . All this is very good; yet . . . you are a goose-cap. Thou art poore, thou wantest favour . . . and therefore art neither to bee heard, nor beleeved. These are not Cases, that are to be brought before the Tribunals of men; but . . . to have thy cause tryed . . . get thee to God . . . where the truth shall appeare face to face . . . (*Rogue*, II, 108)

Guzmán-Alemán invokes God's wrath, declaring that He will punish owners of ill-got gains: "And it shall bee impossible for thee to be saved, by keeping those goods in thy hands which thou hast stolne . . ." (II, 109). It is as though Alemán himself had become God (as indeed he is within the small universe of his novel), and were inflicting eternal damnation on his enemies.

Bearing in mind that Alemán here equates the theft of Guzmán's luggage to Martí's fraudulent *Guzmán*, it follows that Alejandro Bentivoglio is an allegorical representation of some other person connected with the spurious continuation. Two facts stand out concerning Bentivoglio: he is the one who profits most from the pilferage, and he has Guzmán imprisoned. In the Spanish Golden Age, those who enjoyed most of the earnings from literary works were the booksellers who bought the rights from the authors and published their books. The natural person with whom to identify Bentivoglio would seem to be Francisco Miguel, the Valencian bookdealer who paid the publication costs of Martí's *Guzmán*. However, Miguel's biography does not appear to cross that of Mateo Alemán and he may safely be discarded. The other lead for running down the real person behind the name of Alejandro Bentivoglio is provided by Alemán's imprisonment of 1602-1603, which seems to correspond to the unjust punishment suffered by Guzmán. It will be remembered that Alemán was jailed for reneging on a debt to a certain Diego or Miguel López, who may have been in collusion with Francisco López and Miguel Martínez, the publishers of a pirated edition of *Guzmán* (see Chapter 1, Sections XIII-XIV above). Is it possible that López and Martínez urged Juan Martí to write the spurious *Guzmán*, in order to take revenge for the monetary loss that Alemán inflicted on them when he discovered their piracy? And could their piracy in turn have been a means of recovering the money that López had loaned to Alemán and which the latter refused to return? These questions will probably remain unanswered, unless new documents about Alemán's life are uncovered. At any rate, the allegorical import of the Bentivoglio episode seems to be that the novelist was imprisoned for demanding his rights concerning the literary robbery. In other words, it appears that Alemán associates the loan for which he was jailed with the spurious *Guzmán*.

The choice of name of Alejandro Bentivoglio is another intriguing mystery. The Bentivoglio family was a very old and illustrious one in Bologna. In the sixteenth century there was a member of this clan by the name of Alessandro (Alejandro in Spanish). Unlike other masculine members of the family, this Alessandro did nothing of historical note; he is simply mentioned in biographies of the Bentivoglios. However, Alessandro Bentivoglio's name is well known to posterity through the writings of Matteo Bandello, who immortalized Alessandro's wife, Ippolita Sforza, in his novels. Bentivoglio is spoken of some twenty times in Bandello's *Novelle,* a work the creator of Guzmán knew thoroughly. It seems logical to suppose that the name stuck in Alemán's mind as a result of his reading of Bandello. What is not clear is why he selected this name to associate with Martí's *Guzmán.* In this connection it is significant that at about the time Alemán was writing Part II, the bookseller Miguel Martínez published a Spanish version of Bandello's novels (Valladolid, 1603). Could Alemán, by some bizarre association of ideas, have identified Bentivoglio with Miguel Martínez and Francisco López, who may have been partly responsible for the apocryphal *Guzmán*? The problem may never be solved. In any case, it is noteworthy that in 1603 López taunted his enemy Alemán by printing an edition of Martí's *Guzmán.* Another detail that may not be wholly irrelevant is that Alemán emphasizes (II, i, 8) that Alejandro Bentivoglio was named after his father, just as Francisco López was named after his.

VII *Sayavedra, Martí's Protagonist*

The content of Book ii is primarily concerned with a comparison of Guzmán de Alfarache and Sayavedra—that is, the respective protagonists of Alemán's and Martí's novels. To date, critics of *Guzmán* have been almost unanimous in identifying Sayavedra with his creator Juan Martí. However, a perusal of Alemán's novel makes it evident that such is not the case. On two occasions Alemán emphasizes that Martí is Sayavedra's older brother. Sayavedra himself declares this:

> We were two brothers . . . My . . . brother, is somewhat elder than my selfe, and though both of us [had a reasonable subsistence, yet that did not put a bridle on us and] . . . we did agree betweene our selves, to change and alter our names. My brother being a good Latinist, and a fine Scholler, fetched his name, I know not from whence; His owne name being *Iuan Marti*, of *Iuan*, he made *Luxan*; and of *Marti*, *Mateo*; and turning it by inverting the words, he call'd himselfe *Mateo Luxan*. . . . But I, for that I had no learning . . . and knowing that the *Sayavedra's* were of principall note, and ancient Gentlemen of *Sevill*, I stiled my selfe to be of that Citie, and tooke their name upon me. (*Rogue*, II, 128-29)

(The references here to Juan Martí's learning, and Sayavedra's lack of it agree completely with Alemán's prologue, where he talks of the spurious author's erudition, and criticizes his protagonist for being a mediocre student.) In Chapter 5 Guzmán again refers to Sayavedra's "elder brother, *Sennor Iuan Marti*, or *Mateo Luxan* (leaving him to make choyse of one of the two, as shall stand best with his worships liking) . . ." (II, 141), and alludes to Martí's legal profession. This is not to say that there is an absolute dichotomy between creator and character, for Sayavedra's Valencian background and his assumed name are obviously reflections of Martí's.

Critics have heretofore interpreted Sayavedra as representing Martí because his name is the second part of Juan Martí's pseudonym "Mateo Luján de Sayavedra." It is true that Alemán took Sayavedra's name from this source, but he dissociated it from Martí and gave it to his creature. Alemán's choice of cognomen is an excellent example of how names can be used to convey information. "Sayavedra" simultaneously distinguishes Martí's hero from the true Guzmán, shows that he is an impostor, and alludes to Martí; furthermore, it is appropriately a surname used as a first name, like "Guzmán." It is interesting to follow Alemán's creative process for denominating the character and at the same time exposing the spurious author. Alemán first divides the pseudonym into two parts: "Mateo Luján" and "Sayavedra." The second part is the perfect choice for the character, because of the reasons just enumerated. Next the author pretends that Juan Martí chose the pseudonym "Mateo Luján" because it was an anagram of his own name (in reality it was simply a rhyming imitation of "Mateo Alemán"). Then Alemán reverses this formula, changing "Mateo Luján" back into "Juan Martí," and makes the owner of the name a character in his novel.

In other words, Alemán took the pseudonym under which his enemy sought to hide and turned it into an instrument to expose him and to destroy his protagonist. The *nom de plume,* like a cell, divided into two parts, both of which became characters in Alemán's novel. Since these personages had a common matrix in Martí's pseudonym, it was natural that they should be brothers in the novel. From Martí's point of view, the pseudonym became the monster that destroyed Frankenstein. By a reverse process leading from fantasy to reality, the pen name—a projection of Martí's imagination—recoiled and threw the glare of publicity on him.

Worse still for the spurious author, Alemán's mixing of reality and fiction turned Martí into a literary character—that is, a figment of his own imagination. Within the world of Alemán's novel, Juan Martí dissolves into a mere literary reality, subject to the whims of his master. This is strikingly evident when Alemán makes up a spurious biography for Martí (II, ii, 4). Sayavedra says that his brother wandered around Castile and Andalusia in a miserable state, and then went to the Indies,[3] where he also had a bad time of it. The apocryphal author is reduced to the plight of a puppet, and thus is in the same relation to Alemán as his creature Sayavedra.

VIII *Sayavedra, an Autonomous Character*

The appearance of Sayavedra in Part II of Alemán's *Guzmán* is a remarkable case of autonomy in a literary character. It has been shown that the autonomous character is an expression of a typically Spanish attitude: the refusal to distinguish fantasy from reality.[4] This blending of fiction and reality has been characteristic of Spanish literature since the thirteenth century, when the authors of the *Libro de Alexandre* (*Book of Alexander*) and the *Libro de Apolonio* (*Book of Apollonius*) began to detach themselves from their characters. The tendency continued in the late medieval *Cancioneros* (collections of verse), the sentimental novels of Diego de San Pedro (late fifteenth century), the *Sergas de Esplandián* (*Exploits of Esplandián*—the fifth book of *Amadís de Gaula,* composed by Garci Rodríguez de Montalvo in 1508), *La lozana andaluza* (a pornographic novel written in 1524 by Francisco Delicado), and finally *Don Quixote,* where the technique reached its highest expression. Long before Pirandello inverted art and life in his *Six Characters in Search of an Author,* Cervantes had raised Don Quixote from the position of a plain fictional character to that of a person conscious of his extended literary reputation.[5] Don Quixote has at the same time both a novelistic and a real existence. Perhaps the most famous example of Cervantes' technique of interior duplication is in the episode of the puppet show of Maese Pedro, where Don Quixote becomes so convinced of the reality of the action that he injects himself bodily into the world of the marionettes, creating a situation of fiction-within-fiction.

Not known to most critics, there is an even more unusual exemplification of the reversibility of the real and the imaginary in Part II of Mateo Alemán's *Guzmán de Alfarache.* In his autobiography Guzmán relates how he met an impersonator of himself—the protagonist of a false account of his life. This impostor, who now calls himself Sayavedra instead of Guzmán, tells of a rascally brother of his, Juan Martí, who is none other than the author of the spurious biography. Alemán then elevates the literary character to a status superior to that of his creator, for Sayavedra makes up a fictional life for Martí, just as the latter had done to him in the apocryphal *Guzmán*. The parts of author and character are reversed: Sayavedra repudiates the role of impersonator, thus throwing off the chains with which Martí shackled him, and becomes the servant of the real Guzmán de Alfarache. The fusion of art and life is complete: the character first frees himself from his creator, rejecting a role he does not wish to play, and then reduces his author to the level of fiction. Reality is so subtly amalgamated with fantasy that the reader is perplexed as to which characters represent real people and which are purely literary creatures. Palpable proof of this is that to date scholars have confused the character Sayavedra with his author Juan Martí.

IX *A Comparison of Guzmán and Sayavedra*

The adventures in Book ii are designed to prove the intellectual superiority of Guzmán to Sayavedra. Alemán's hero tortures his wits to contrive ingenious schemes that will dazzle Sayavedra and show up his lack of ingenuity. The author foreshadows this purpose in his prologue, where he scoffs at Sayavedra's gaucherie: "he could not be called a most famous theefe, for the stealing of three cloakes, howbeit two of them were very faire ones, and of much value, but the other a poore one" (*Rogue*, II, **3)—an allusion to the last chapter of Martí's novel.

Alemán's principal ally in demonstrating the preeminence of his hero is Martí himself. In the apocryphal *Guzmán* the protagonist admits that two roguish companions "doubtless were more crafty and expert than I" (i, 1)—an admission inconceivable in the authentic Guzmán—and on another occasion naïvely boasts that he "was not completely stupid" (i, 3). Martí's rogue never displays the slightest spark of originality in his antisocial activities. While the true Guzmán uses imaginative deceits to commit important robberies, Martí's picaro does nothing more clever than filching kitchen scraps, snatching capes, or stealing clothes from an absent owner.

Alemán makes Martí's protagonist an equally drab figure in the authentic continuation. Sayavedra's only independent crime is the theft of his friend's luggage, accomplished by falsifying some keys and impersonating Guzmán (II, i, 8). Sayavedra is the first to admit his inferiority: on meeting Guzmán after his release from prison, Sayavedra throws himself at his feet and begs to be accepted as a slave (II, ii, 1). Guzmán generously forgives his betrayal of faith and takes him into his service. Sayavedra immediately proves to be faint-hearted, preferring not to become involved in the case against Alejandro Bentivoglio (II, ii, 2). Thereafter he assists Guzmán in his cheats at cards (II, ii, 3) and gapes with amazement at the master rogue's ingenuity in victimizing a usurer in Milan (II, ii, 5-6).

Guzmán is ever emphasizing his own expertise and contrasting it with Sayavedra's inadequacies. Of himself Guzmán says: "When any doubts did arise, I did resolve them; if they were to seeke for Plots, I did invent them: and in all weghty businesses, I [presided] . . ." (*Rogue,* II, 168). Sayavedra, on the other hand, is only a sneak thief; Guzmán advises his lackey to raise his sights:

> I would not have thee busie thy selfe in base thefts, nor be none of those sneaking theeves, that steale Primers, Horne-bookes and Ballads; for from such kinde of thefts, thou shalt reape no other profit, but infamie, and reproach. (II, 127)

After a brilliant theft, Guzmán observes:

> *Sayavedra,* though he felt it, had it in his hands . . . yet could he not beleeve it was there. . . . I said then unto him; friend *Sayavedra*; This is true knowledge . . . to steale without danger . . . and thrive well by it. As for those things which thou didst preach unto mee upon the way, they were lessons of the *Turkish Alcoran* . . . To steale a kirtle, and receive a hundred stripes for it, every foole can doe this. (II, 158-59)

In Chapter 5 Guzmán concludes that Sayavedra "was an unfortunate pilchard . . . and I, in comparison of him, a . . . Whale" (II, 141).

In II, ii, 4, Alemán has Martí's protagonist tell of his past, particularly his adventures in Italy previous to meeting Guzmán. It would appear logical that these adventures be a résumé of the action of the apocryphal *Guzmán,* but such is not the case.

Alemán invents a false biography for Martí's character, turning the tables on his imitator. Sayavedra claims that he was one of the most accomplished petty thieves in Naples. He recounts how he used to enter stables to pilfer mule blankets, currycombs, or sieves; if someone entered, he lowered his trousers and pretended to be engaged in a necessity of nature. Crowds were also good places to practice his art, for there daggers, handkerchiefs, purses, rosaries, women's jewels, and children's trinkets were to be had; and if worse came to worse, Sayavedra could cut pieces from men's capes, to use for patching stockings. Other thefts garnered a skirt, some candlesticks, and a couple of shirts; this last pilferage occasioned imprisonment, a beating, and exile from Naples. In addition to mocking Martí, Sayavedra's narration seems to have a twofold purpose: Alemán first pictures Martí's character as incapable of conceiving the clever robberies in which Guzmán excels; and secondly, Alemán demonstrates his superior inventive abilities, fabricating petty thefts much more interesting than Martí's.

Because of his unchallenged primacy over his rival, Guzmán can afford to be condescendent and take a protective attitude toward Sayavedra. When the latter feels compunction for his disloyal conduct, Guzmán benevolently insists that bygones be bygones, and shares his booty equally with his servant (II, ii, 4). But he always keeps aloof from Sayavedra, reminding him of the distance between master and lackey (II, ii, 3). Sayavedra has such great admiration for Guzmán that he adopts his name at the end of Chapter 6. Martí's protagonist is mute from respect during Chapters 7-8, where Guzmán takes revenge on his cruel uncle and other relatives who scorned him seven years earlier. These deceits are perhaps the most elaborate in the novel, meant as an appropriate retaliation for the treatment Guzmán received in Part II, iii, 1, and offering convincing evidence of Alemán's superiority over Martí, since the latter had forgotten Guzmán's vow to avenge himself. Alemán's hero prefaces his reprisal with a jibe addressed to his servitor: "if thou *Sayavedra* wert [as thou likest to think] . . . thou wouldst ere this have been at *Genoa*, and have revenged the wrong that I there received" (*Rogue*, II, 160).

In Chapter 9 Guzmán and Sayavedra embark for Spain with

the riches acquired in their last adventures. Sayavedra loses his mind from fright during a tempest; while the other passengers pray for deliverance, he cries: "I am *Guzman de Alfarache*'s ghost; I am that ghost of his, which goes thus wandring up and downe the world" (II, 193). He then alludes to his past life—that is, as it appears in Martí's novel. The night after the storm, he casts himself into the sea and drowns. Guzmán inwardly rejoices at the death of his impersonator, but to keep up appearances feigns grief. Sayavedra's suicide is an eerie type of literary sorcery; it suggests that Alemán would like to sink the apocryphal character (and his creator) into deepest Hell, but exempts him from this fate by making him go out of his mind, which, as is well known, removes responsibility for the mortal sin of suicide, according to Catholic doctrine. The elimination of Sayavedra seems to disclose a mixture of hate and pity in Alemán's mind: hate for the lack of scruples displayed by Sayavedra and his inventor, and pity for their want of talent.

Sayavedra's suicide is not unique in Spanish literature, in that other authors have killed characters they took from other novels. For example, in Juan de Flores' *Grimalte y Gradissa* (1495?), a continuation of Boccaccio's *Fiammetta,* the Italian heroine takes her own life. However, the cases are different, for Flores treats Boccaccio's character as if she were his own, and does not place a curse on her, as does Alemán on Sayavedra.

It may seem strange that Alemán chose to vent his fury against Sayavedra, the creature, rather than against Martí, the creator. The reason possibly lies in the author's great rage and bitterness: he wished to take an exquisite and protracted revenge. Had he spoken directly against the imitator, he either would have had to confine his remarks to the prologue, or introduce himself directly into the novel, breaking the literary illusion. Alemán chose the more artistic alternative of withdrawing (in the prologue he does not even mention Martí's name) and letting his protagonist take prolonged vengeance of his novelistic opposite, Sayavedra. In order to do this, Alemán acknowledges that in the world of the novel, Martí's hero is just as real a being as his own. The distinction between fiction and existence is wiped out, as the apocryphal character comes alive and wanders about with Guzmán. Starting from this point, Alemán proceeds to demonstrate that Martí's protagonist is infinitely inferior to his own. The Sevillian admits the reality of his enemy's hero only with the sadistic purpose of destroying him, first in reputation and then literally.

Cervantes employs a similar technique when he introduces into his novel (II, 72) a character from Avellaneda's spurious continuation and makes him confess that the Don Quixote and Sancho that he knows are impersonators. In an earlier chapter (II, 59), Cervantes has his characters treat the false *Quixote* as a work of literature existing on a different level of reality from themselves, thus creating the situation of fiction-within-fiction.

Critics of *Guzmán de Alfarache* have commonly affirmed that Mateo Alemán did not treat Juan Martí with the severity that Cervantes showed toward his pseudonymous imitator, "Alonso Fernández de Avellaneda." Nothing could be farther from the truth. Cervantes makes numerous allusions to Avellaneda, but always with the restraint that characterizes his thought. This is a far cry from the flaying that Alemán administers to Martí. The picaresque novelist devotes two paragraphs of his dedication to an arraignment of his imitator, writes a special prologue ("Reader") to point up the defects of the spurious continuation, and employs roughly a third of his Part II in satirizing Martí and his protagonist. Alemán's bitterness is justified, for Martí did more than write an apocryphal continuation, like Avellaneda; much graver was his betrayal of faith and theft of Alemán's ideas.

CHAPTER 6

Part II of Guzmán: *Conclusion*

I *The* Arancel de necedades

BOOK iii of Part II is one of the most compressed in the entire novel; besides being packed with adventures, it contains nineteen interpolated tales and about a dozen digressions. However, it is not one of the most original books; the necessity of finishing the continuation in a minimum of time forced Alemán to follow written sources and to repeat himself occasionally.

Upon Guzmán's return to Spain, Alemán has him journey to Saragossa, where he takes lodging at an inn. On blowing his nose, the rogue is informed by his jovial host that he has lost a forfeit. Guzmán's offense consists in contemplating his handkerchief after using it—one of the many ridiculous customs penalized by the innkeeper in a code he has drawn up, entitled *Arancel de necedades* (Mabbe renders it "The statutes and constitutions of *Gotam Colledge*: or The Hospitall of Fooles"). Some of the persons who fall under the penalties of these statutes are: those who walk along the lines formed by the paving stones on streets; those who spit from a high place attempting to strike a particular object; "They, who blowing their nose, in the taking away of their handkercher, looke steadily upon it, and pry into it, as if some pearles had dropt from thence, and that they would safely lay them up for feare of losing [them] . . ." (*Rogue*, II, 221); and many others. When the innkeeper observes an individual practicing one of these idle diversions, he charges him a fee and initiates him into a brotherhood of simpletons governed by the mock code.

Alemán's *Arancel de necedades* became so popular that it was published separately in Valencia in 1615. It was included, along with additional silly mannerisms, in the *Premáticas y aranceles generales* (*General Pragmatic Sanctions and Tariffs*—a title that parodies the many official pronouncements made in Golden Age Spain), another collection of foibles compiled for the entertainment of careless society. The *Premáticas* circulated widely in manuscript form in the seventeenth century, and are commonly attributed not to Alemán but to Francisco de Quevedo. The authorship is still in doubt; scholars have been unable to decide whether Quevedo took his statutes from Alemán, or vice versa, or whether perhaps both writers took them from a common source. The last hypothesis seems the most probable. Alemán's version antedates Quevedo's, but in view of the fact that most of the interpolated material in Part II of *Guzmán* can be traced to known sources, it seems unlikely that Alemán wrote the original statutes. Guzmán says that he reproduces only a selection from his host's extensive tabulation; this intimates that Alemán took fragments from a longer document. It is quite possible that satirical rules of etiquette like the *Arancel* actually existed toward the end of the sixteenth century in taverns and other places of reunion for travelers and loafers—just as in *Guzmán*. The rogue's partial reproduction of the innkeeper's compilation of follies was likely based on such a manuscript, and thus was the first literary version of a long popular tradition. The author of the published *Premáticas y aranceles generales*—Quevedo or someone else—probably reproduced a manuscript in its entirety.

Alemán's *Arancel de necedades* and the probable folkloric tradition that it reflects are related to a type of book in vogue in Europe during the sixteenth and seventeenth centuries: the parody of courtesy literature. Like the *Arancel*, these treatises poke fun at the handbooks of genteel deportment which had become so influential in Italy, Spain, France, and England after the publication of Baldesar Castiglione's *The Courtier* (1528). Perhaps the most famous satirical treatment of rules of conduct was the Italian Giovanni della Casa's *Galateo* (1550-1555), adapted into Spanish by Lucas Gracián Dantisco under the title of *Galateo español* (1582). This extremely popular book criticizes the same bad habit for which Guzmán pays a fine to the innkeeper, and so could well be an indirect source of Alemán's *Arancel*.[1]

II *Amorous Adventures*

In Saragossa Guzmán falls in love with a beautiful widow, although local custom decrees that women may marry only once. With his thoughts on love, Guzmán goes about the city by night. He meets a bold prostitute who cozens him by picking his pockets while allowing him to dally with her. She promises Guzmán an assignation, but does not open the door. Later the rogue converses with a wench at a window. A dog begins to bark at him, interrupting the interview. The picaro goes to pick up a stone to throw at the animal, but instead grasps some filth. As usual, Guzmán's love affairs end unhappily and scatalogically. The scene in which a character besmears himself was a favorite in Golden Age literature; Alemán's good friend Lope de Vega included a similar comic scene in his lighthearted play *Las ferias de Madrid* (*The Fairs in Madrid*), composed around 1588.[2] The amorous adventure with the streetwalker is reminiscent of Part I, ii, 8, where another courtesan had deceived the rogue. The obscene portion of the episode is similar to Guzmán's mishaps in Part II, i, 5-6, since in both cases the picaro gets befouled through the fault of an animal while courting.

Alemán's self-plagiarism continues in Chapter 2, where a description of Guzmán's preenings and struttings before his lady's house imitates closely a passage from Part I, ii, 8.[3] There are further parallels between the love entanglements of Parts I and II of *Guzmán*. In the first part of the novel, after carrying on some disastrous courtships in Toledo, Guzmán moves on to Malagón and there too becomes involved with a wench. The same general action occurs in the continuation: the rogue leaves Saragossa after the streetwalker who deceived him has fallen into the hands of the law (cf. the ending of the first adventure in I, ii, 8), and goes to Madrid, where he has an affair with a young woman. When he refuses to buy her an unusually expensive gift, the siren and her mother have Guzmán arrested for constupration and he is forced to make a costly settlement. Guzmán subsequently learns that this is the third time that the lady has sued for loss of virginity.

This chicanery moves Alemán to consider at length the problem of scheming females who ensnare husbands or win large payments on false charges of rape. The picaresque novelist concludes that "No force of man can prevaile against the woman that is unwilling" (*Rogue*, II, 236). This issue was later treated by many other Golden Age authors, who accepted Alemán's conclusions. The question provoked extensive comment in the theater: Lope de Vega, Tirso de Molina, Vélez de Guevara, and Pérez de Montalbán all mentioned it in one or more plays.[4]

Alemán dwells at length on the subject of the injustice done to men forced to marry women who yielded themselves freely. He ridicules the concept of rape and points out the immorality of weddings based on it:

> But say such a thing might once in a thousand yeares chance to happen; me thinkes it is no reason, that a businesse of this nature should be compounded withall for money, much lesse injoyne them marriage, (unlesse he had formerly given her his word and faithfull promise before witnesses) but that in this case, the fittest meanes, were personall punishment . . . by this meanes, men would have more feare, and women more shame . . . (*Rogue*, II, 236-37)

The embittered sincerity of these observations reveals that Guzmán is speaking for his creator. Mateo Alemán vents his rage against his wife Catalina, who had forced him into marriage.

III *Marriage*

The remainder of Chapter 2 contains many autobiographical elements intermingled with adventures. Like Alemán, Guzmán buys a lot in Madrid, on which he must pay an annuity, and builds a house. The rogue sells some jewels he stole from his Genoese uncle and with this capital becomes a merchant and usurer. His well-being is temporary, however, for he suddenly marries a girl who spends excessively until they are bankrupt. Guzmán's father-in-law teaches him sharp practices—tricks similar to those in which Mateo Alemán doubtless engaged, either as defrauder or victim. Thanks to fake bills of debt and counterbills of credit, the picaro manages to escape from his bankruptcy with minimum losses. Alemán fulminates against the widespread use by merchants of false deeds and counter-writings, which enable borrowers to renege on their obligations with impunity. It is entirely possible that the novelist had lost money as a result of these manipulations.

Chapter 3 is devoted to two long digressions, one against usury—to which Alemán often had fallen victim—and the other against women who make their husbands miserable—no doubt a reference to the writer's wife, Catalina. Guzmán's spouse accuses him of keeping a mistress—surely one of the complaints Alemán faced—and constantly complains about the scarcity of spending money, a perennial problem in the novelist's household. Guzmán-Alemán depicts himself as a patient and long-suffering husband. After six years of wretched married life, Guzmán's wife dies "of a sharpe disease, without shewing any tokens of repentance, or receiving the Sacrament" (*Rogue,* II, 264). This consignment to Hell is an even more severe fate than that visited on Sayavedra, for the latter escaped damnation through his insanity.

To conclude the philippic against his wife, Guzmán-Alemán tells a short tale: During a storm the master of a ship instructs the passengers to throw overboard their heaviest possessions in order to lighten the vessel. A distressed husband tosses his wife into the sea, claiming that "amongst all the marchandize hee had aboord, there was not any that weighed so heavie as his wife . . ." (II, 265). Alemán had probably read this popular story in Melchor de Santa Cruz' *Floresta española* (*A Spanish Literary Forest*) IX, iv, 6, and in Domenichi's *Facezie* (ed. cit., No. 136).

In the last chapter of the novel, Guzmán returns to the subject of marriage and takes a more objective view, recognizing that matrimony can be a happy state: ". . . a good and peaceable mariage, where love, and condition of the parties stand upon equall termes, it is a glory; it is an enjoyning both of earth and Heaven . . ." (II, 349). However, the rogue also describes the other side of the coin, illustrating it with an anecdote. A Provençal, "being quite wearyed and tyred out with a shrewd Wife," decides to rid himself of her. He invites her to an outing and has her mount a mule that has drunk no water in three days. On approaching a river, the thirst-crazed animal plunges into the water and the wife is drowned. This tale was widely diffused in Alemán's day; the novelist could have read it in Santa Cruz, Giraldi Cinthio, Guicciardini, or Doni. Lope de

Vega later included it in his play *El príncipe perfecto* (*The Perfect Prince*), Part II.[5]

IV *University Studies*

In Chapter 4 Guzmán resolves to sell his house and to follow a religious vocation. The chapter begins with two extended digressions: one against those who, like Guzmán, study for the priesthood only with the purpose of assuring themselves an easy living; and another protesting against the system of yearly rents, which stipulated that when a piece of property was sold, the holder of the rent received a twentieth of the selling price, regardless of the original value of the real estate. Mateo Alemán doubtless suffered financial loss under this arrangement (there were four such encumbrances on his house in Madrid), and therefore he complains acrimoniously about its unfairness.

After disposing of his house, Guzmán departs for the University of Alcalá de Henares, where he takes up residence in a boarding house. In a very amusing passage, the picaro describes the eternal bone of contention among students—the food at college. Alemán's portrayal of the starvation diet rationed out to students was later carried to the ultimate extreme of stylization by Quevedo in his *Buscón* (i, 3). The descriptions of a cheese dessert and a pea soup suffice to give an idea of Alemán's artistry:

> For our last course . . . we had a thinne slice of cheese, which seemed . . . like those thinne shavings which your joyners planish away with their plainers . . . [The boarding-house keeper alleged] that those thicker slunchins would dull our wits. Besides, it was so full of eyes, and so transparent, that whosoever had seene it, would have judg'd it to have beene . . . some Lambkins mid-riffe . . . And upon fish-dayes, wee had a messe of lentill porrige, such as *AEsope* was fed withall [i.e., with one lentil] . . . I assure you, that the best and cunningest *Indian*-diver of them all, that fishes for Pearles, must have bin forced to have dived foure times at least, to the bottome of my porringer, before he should be able to bring up one of these pearles . . . (*Rogue*, II, 274-75)

It is likely that the inspiration for these descriptions came from Santa Cruz' *Floresta* (IV, viii, 4-5), where a student undresses to dive for a pea at the bottom of his porringer, and covers his mouth so as not to blow away the cheese dessert with his breath.

Guzmán has a merry time at college, snatching pastries and sweetmeats, giving serenades, harassing freshmen, and rigging student elections. At the same time he does very well in his studies, standing first in his class, although at graduation this honor is unjustly conferred on an influential gentleman's son (a similar type of injustice is later done to Tomás Rodaja, the protagonist of Cervantes' *Licenciado Vidriera* [*Licentiate of Glass*]). After seven years of study, when only a few months remain until his ordination, the rogue becomes enamored of Gracia, an innkeeper's daughter, and marries her.

V *Views on Love. Second Marriage*

Chapter 5 begins with a long essay on the defects of love between man and woman. Alemán believes that the blindness that characterizes love was caused by original sin:

> After mans first sinne . . . our passions and affections having got the upper-hand, and we being furthered and led along with a blinde and depraved understanding, and hungring and thirsting after our owne lustfull appetites, we doe inconsiderately debase our manly brests . . . (*Rogue*, II, 290)

This is one reason why Guzmán fell in love with Gracia at first sight. Another contributing factor is astral influence:

> That for a man to fall in love, there is no such force or necessity in it . . . but that upon the very first view . . . there may jointly concurre in both, a correspondency . . . a conformity of the bloud, wherein the starres by a particular influence, are wont to worke . . . (II, 289)

Elsewhere in his novel (I, iii, 10), Alemán makes clear that he shares the typical seventeenth century opinion that the stars incline but do not compel man's free will.[6] Alemán's obeisance to Classical ideas (the suggestion that stars influence man's destiny) at the same time that he affirms Catholic doctrine (original sin, free will) reflects the characteristically Renaissance ability to reconcile two antithetic concepts.

The idea here presented of love is a deformed one. Alemán reduces love to an exclusively physical passion, terming it "an excess of bestial cupidity." The simplistic explanation that love is a result of the First Fall is not even good theology, for it tends to ignore the individual's free will and responsibility. The novelist incurs the error of believing that any part of love that is not absolutely spiritual is sinful. He goes so far as to condemn women, blaming them for being the cause of man's sin. Alemán's failure to recognize the legitimate place of physical love in marriage is probably a result of his feelings of guilt in his extramarital affairs, and also of the prevalence in Spain at this time of the exaggerated Augustinian ideal of celibacy for all statuses.[7] Events in Alemán's life caused him to give in Part II a much more negative view of love than that of Part I (i, 2), where he placed conjugal affection next to love for God, and above friendship (*Rogue,* I, 21).

Having condemned love, Guzmán proceeds to narrate the story of his second marriage. Things go very well at first, for the rogue's in-laws regard him highly and wait on him hand and foot. But the family falls on hard times after the death of Gracia's father. Guzmán takes up his studies again, following a different specialization, but soon has to abandon them—another coincidence with Alemán's biography (in the year 1580).

To make a living, Guzmán panders for his wife—a not uncommon practice in Spain during the seventeenth century, according to contemporary literature. Guzmán's predecessor, Lazarillo de Tormes, had also been a complacent husband, marrying a servant who was the paramour of an archpriest. As usual in his imitations of *Lazarillo,* Alemán elaborates on his model, introducing variations on the basic theme. Whereas Lazarillo's wife had only one lover who helped support the household in a modest way, Gracia attracts a number of gallants, and they eventually fill Guzmán's home with all sorts of luxuries. Students' allowances being small, Guzmán and his wife soon desert Alcalá de Henares for Madrid. There Gracia successively exploits a clothier, a rich foreigner, some magnates, and a judge. Finally, their scandalous ways cause Guzmán's and Gracia's banishment, and they move to Seville.

VI *Hard Times. New Swindles*

The picaro's involvement with prostitution brings him into contact with his mother, of whom he had had no news since his departure many years before. Her beauty long vanished, she now peddles the favors of a girl she has reared. Guzmán persuades his mother to live with him and to instruct his wife in the finer points of her profession. The old go-between gives Gracia good counsel, teaching her what kinds of suitors to admit to her company. Unfortunately for Guzmán, the two women do not get along, and Gracia runs off to Italy with their most precious possessions. The rogue takes this reverse in stride, reasoning that "he is a Mad-man, or a Foole, that will seeke after his Wife, when she is once gone: And that a man should make a golden Bridge, for a flying enemy . . ." (*Rogue,* II, 312). These same thoughts were later expressed by Cervantes in *El Licenciado Vidriera, El casamiento engañoso* (*The Deceitful Marriage*), and *Persiles y Sigismunda* (Book iii, Chapter 7).

After losing his source of income, Guzmán resorts to petty theft. Among other activities, he snatches capes and makes them into doublets with the help of his mother. The latter is not pleased with this trade, being unwilling to run the risk of "so foule an affront" (II, 313), and returns to her former occupation of pandering. Guzmán subsequently offers to guard a house and sells every removable object from it, including the tiles from the roof. One day he picks a gentleman's pocket, but the coins fall to the street. The quick-thinking rogue pretends that the money fell from his own pocket when he pulled out a handkerchief, and the gentleman helps him pick it up. This episode is probably an imitation of Timoneda's *Buen aviso* (II, 96). In another clever trick, Guzmán takes to a saintly priest a purse he avers to have found, thereby impressing the cleric with his honesty; the picaro's mother claims the pocketbook and the friar collects a generous donation for Guzmán from his congregation. This swindle appears in Masuccio Salernitano's *Novellino,* tale 16.

With a view toward emigrating to the Indies (an ideal of New Christians both real and literary, e.g., Alemán and Quevedo's Pablos), Guzmán embezzles a large sum, which he gives for safekeeping to his mother. However, he is caught, imprisoned, and sentenced to the galleys for six years. His term is increased to life after an abortive attempt to escape from jail dressed as a woman. The rogue's mother keeps all the goods he had entrusted to her.

A large part of Chapter 7 is devoted to a criticism of prison life, as had been promised in Book ii, 3. Guzmán points up the venality of jailers and lawyers, who exploit the prisoners pitilessly. Although Alemán's imprisonment of December, 1602, was still fresh in his mind, this particular passage reveals the influence of Cristóbal de Chaves' *Relación de la cárcel de Sevilla* (*Account of the Prison of Seville*),[8] composed between 1585 and 1597. It seems likely that the earlier digression against prison officials and ministers of justice (II, ii, 3) reflects the author's personal experience of 1602-1603, and that the present digression was written before that time. Indeed, there is evidence that this portion of Chapter 7 may have been part of Alemán's first draft of his continuation. Martí's description of a jail in Book i, 7 of the apocryphal *Guzmán* is quite similar to Alemán's and could well have been based on it. An instance of poor craftsmanship also indicates that Alemán hurriedly adapted this chapter from an earlier draft; he assumes that the reader is acquainted with several characters (Juliana, Soto and Gómez) who have not appeared previously in the novel. One of these characters, Soto, plays a key part in the last chapter of Part II. Since Guzmán repeatedly refers to Soto as "my Camerade," it seems that they were friends in the first version. In sum, it is probable that Alemán interpolated into his revision fragments from the original version of the continuation, without making sure that they fitted in with the new material. This careless work is likely attributable to Alemán's need to meet a printer's deadline.

VII *Guzmán's Mother*

An intriguing sidelight of Chapters 6-8 of Book iii is the reappearance of Guzmán's mother (see Chapter 4, Section III above).

As was mentioned earlier, the typical picaro begins his story with a humorous or satirical account of his parents' life histories. In *Lazarillo de Tormes,* the rogue's progenitors occupy only the first few pages and then disappear from view. Alemán, on the other hand, reintroduces Guzmán's mother in the final chapters of his work and goes much further in his scoffing at the venerated figure of the parent.

If Guzmán's mother was a woman of loose morals in her younger days (Part I, i, 2), she is now even less respectable, if that is possible. Having passed the age of promiscuity, she lives off the earnings of an adopted daughter, also a prostitute. The sage and cynical advice she gives her daughter-in-law (II, iii, 6) is a distillation of her extensive experience in the service of Venus. Guzmán's mother is of a venal and calculating sort. Although she helps her son for a time in his petty larcenies after Gracia's desertion, she too leaves him when it is apparent that the profits are small. As Guzmán's fortunes look up and he steals considerable amounts, his mother serves as a depositary —only to appropriate the money to herself. The rogue's last words concerning his mother, though brief, are among the most condemnatory. The occasion is the picaro's transfer from the prison in Seville to the galleys—the last opportunity for mother and son to see each other, because of Guzmán's life sentence. She evinces absolutely no maternal sentiments; the rogue observes that "my mother did not come to accompany me, nor was she willing to see me. And I was the only man amongst them all, that was . . . left alone to my selfe" (*Rogue,* II, 333).

There are several possible explanations for Alemán's negative portrayal of the mother of his protagonist. One is that it is merely a continuation of the unfavorable depiction in Part I, and therefore is merely a literary motif. Another possibility is that Alemán harbored resentment toward his own mother and gave it literary expression, just as he had done with other personal animosities. It is interesting that in the theater of Alemán's friend Lope de Vega there are several dislikable mothers, although this is not usually construed as a reflection of the dramatist's sentiments toward his own mother.[9] In any case, it seems clear that Guzmán's misgivings are the point of departure for the antagonism that Quevedo's protagonist feels toward his parents in *El Buscón.*

Part II of Guzmán: *Conclusion*

VIII *A Galley Slave*

In Chapter 8 Guzmán is marched off to the galleys with other delinquents. He has ample time to meditate, and begins to consider the good of his soul:

Then did I begin to thinke with my selfe; if this be so painefull unto mee already; if this chaine doe so much torment me, that I can scarce indure it . . . What torment will they feele that are condemned for ever to a perpetuall paine? (*Rogue*, II, 332-33)

As before, however, Guzmán's preoccupation with the afterlife does not keep him from committing petty thefts along the way to the galleys. His companion Soto in turn steals from Guzmán and on being discovered, becomes his mortal enemy. On board ship, the rogue again is robbed (in Part II Alemán has a tendency to repeat episodes). The chapter concludes with another attack of conscience. Guzmán echoes the age-old exhortations to awaken from the dream of worldly pleasures; his admonition closely resembles that of the beginning of Jorge Manrique's famous *Coplas a la muerte de su padre* (*Couplets to the Death of his Father*): "Rouze up thy selfe therefore, and awake from thy heavie sleepe, which oppresseth thy soule; Returne home unto thy selfe; and consider . . . Thou hast sought after a stocke to imploy it for thy profit; seeke how to obtaine eternall happinesse . . ." (II, 344). Guzmán has finally arrived at that state of perfection to which Alemán refers in the prologue to the continuation. No Part III is needed, for Guzmán's conversion is sincere and complete:

In this discourse with my selfe . . . I spent a great part of the night, showring downe teares in aboundance . . . I fell asleepe; and when I awak'd, I found my selfe another manner of man . . . I gave thankes unto God for this my regeneration . . . humbly beseeching him, that he would uphold me with his holy hand . . . (II, 344)[10]

Guzmán remains steadfast to his purpose in Chapter 9: "For I was so truely become another man . . . that I would rather suffer my selfe to be torne in a thousand pieces, then to commit any the least crime in the world"; "I had put on a full resolution, not to doe any thing that was infamous, or ill, no not for any profit or benefit that should accrue thereby unto mee . . ." (II, 353, 356).

It has been objected that Guzmán's redemption at the conclusion of the novel is not in keeping with the picaresque tradition, which establishes the open ending, susceptible of further sequels containing roguish adventures. There are several reasons why Guzmán repents at the end. The most obvious is Alemán's moral purpose: his protagonist leads a life of sin, but must be saved to set an example. This ending is likewise necessary in order to justify the insertion of the moralizations throughout the novel; Guzmán must reform before he begins to write his autobiography. Thus Alemán justifies his dual protagonist: the young rogue interested only in having a good time, and the older man who wishes to teach a moral lesson. Then too Alemán wished to guarantee that his protagonist would not be resuscitated in further continuations like that of Juan Martí. After Guzmán's conversion it was no longer possible for him to take up again his picaresque wanderings.[11]

IX *Conclusion*

Guzmán's diligence and honesty come to the attention of his superiors. He becomes the trusted servant of the boatswain and then of a gentleman. The vengeful Soto has an object stolen so Guzmán will be held responsible. Later a hatband of great worth disappears and the protagonist is assumed to be guilty. He is tortured and demoted to the lowest duties on the ship. He overcomes these adversities with his virtue, however. Soto plans a mutiny for which Guzmán's collaboration is necessary. The reformed picaro denounces the uprising, and is rewarded with freedom to move at will about the ship. Still more importantly, he is promised full pardon.

Soto confesses under torture his part as a ringleader in the rebellion; he also divulges, in Guzmán's words, that "his purpose and resolution was when they had made themselves Masters of the Galley, to have stab'd me, his hatred being such towards me, that nothing could satisfie it, but my death" (*Rogue,* II, 357). Soto's punishment consists in being "drawne in peeces with foure Gallies . . ." This severe penalty is reminiscent of those inflicted by Alemán on Sayavedra and on Guzmán's first wife; it therefore seems possible that Soto represents another of the novelist's personal enemies. Earlier Guzmán describes Soto as "the greatest, and most notorious thiefe, that ever was heard of in his time, either in all *Italy,* or in *Spaine*" (II, 355).

Guzmán de Alfarache appropriately ends on a Christian note of hope:

> And here . . . doe I put a full point to these my mis-fortunes, I have given thee a large account of my lewd life . . . What it was hereafter, thou shalt see in my third and last Part, if God shall give me life: and that I doe not first exchange this transitory one, for one that is eternall, which is the hope and life of the faithfull. (II, 357)

X *Part III of* Guzmán

In the prologue of his continuation, Alemán claims to have finished a Part III of *Guzmán,* and he alludes to it again in the final sentence of the novel. But the writer did not publish this Part III in the eleven years that he is known to have lived after making the statement, although he did publish two major works and a minor one during this interval. Guzmán's life is complete at the end of Part II. He has done all that Alemán promised in "A declaration for the better understanding of this Booke" (prologue to Part I), where it is stated that the picaro returns to Spain from Italy, commences studies for the priesthood, becomes "a most famous Thiefe," and being caught and punished, now "writeth his owne life from a-boord the Galleys . . ." (*Rogue,* I, A). Thus the ending of *Guzmán,* as Alemán conceived it throughout Part I, was to be his imprisonment on a galley, the situation in which Part II leaves him.

Alemán's mention of a Part III was prompted solely by Martí's promise of another continuation; the creator of Guzmán de Alfarache never intended to pen a third part except in the event that the Valencian (or another) wrote a second spurious continuation. In the prologue to his continuation, Alemán declares that if Martí publishes a Part III, he will answer it, just as he replied to his Part II. In the same place, Alemán avows the purpose of creating a perfect man from the rogue, after the latter has descended to the most abject misery, which is existence on a galley. Presumably, this would have been the subject of Part III. Such a continuation would have departed greatly from Alemán's original thought, and would not have been picaresque. In light of this, it is better that he did not have to write a Part III.

It is a pity that Alemán, writing in haste, imitated Martí's offer of a new continuation and thereby fell into a contradiction. Autobiographical novels must end at the moment the protagonist pens them, and throughout the work Guzmán has reiterated that he is writing from a galley (see the prologue of Part I; I, i, 1; iii, 5; II, i, 1); therefore, when he refers to subsequent adventures, he is alluding to events in the future, of which he can have no knowledge. Many scholars have taken seriously Mateo Alemán's offer of a Part III, not realizing the conditions under which he made it. In this connection it will be recalled that Cervantes on several occasions promised a continuation of his *Galatea,* but wrote many other works, including *Don Quixote,* without returning to his pastoral novel.

CHAPTER 7

The Interpolated Novelettes in Guzmán

I *Introduction*

TO PROVIDE contrast with Guzmán's picaresque adventures, Mateo Alemán interpolated four independent stories in his novel. The custom of intercalating detachable tales in a longer work of fiction was as old as the Spanish novel itself, dating back to the medieval books of chivalry. And even long before that, it was a common technique in the Classical epic and novel. The interpolated tale was a particularly popular device during Spain's Golden Age, both in the novel and in the drama.[1] It was usually employed in novels of an episodic nature, where the protagonist faced a long series of adventures. The episodic novel could easily become monotonous and consequently put its author's skill to a severe test. To hold his audience's interest, the novelist looked for ways to divert attention from the principal character, while the latter took a rest offstage. The usual solution was to introduce digressions or secondary plots unrelated to the protagonist. As is well known, Cervantes utilized this technique extensively in Part I of *Don Quixote*; in Chapter 44 of his continuation, he defended the device against its critics, but he used it more sparingly in Part II.

Alemán's stories are completely detachable from the main narrative—they are related by walk-on characters introduced for this sole purpose. *Ozmín and Daraja* is narrated by a cleric who disappears shortly after finishing his story. *Dorido and Clorinia* and *Don Luis de Castro* are recited by César, a Neapolitan dinner guest of the French Ambassador, Guzmán's master. It is interesting that César promises to tell more of Dorido's misfortunes, but vanishes without doing so. Perhaps Alemán had planned a continuation of this tale, but under the pressure of publishing Part II rapidly, resorted to the quicker expedient of making adaptations from Masuccio Salernitano. The circumstance that César is a Neapolitan is perhaps an unconscious recollection that Masuccio was from Naples. *Bonifacio and Dorotea* is read to Guzmán and his ship companions from a manuscript; it will be remembered that Cervantes' *Curioso impertinente* (*One Who was too Curious for his Own Good*) is likewise read from papers left in an inn (*Don Quixote,* I, 32).

There is a basic unity in Alemán's novelettes, for they all treat the theme of love—a topic largely excluded from the body of *Guzmán de Alfarache.* Each story views the subject from a different angle, but with an underlying moral intention. Thus the novelettes share with *Guzmán* the purpose of entertaining and edifying at the same time.

Always an adroit narrator seeking to please his readers, Alemán constructed his exemplary stories with elements from diverse types of literature popular in the day: the Greek novel, the Moorish novel, courtly literature, and the Italian *novella. Ozmín and Daraja* is a Moorish novelette based on Heliodorus' *Ethiopian History*; its theme is chaste love, which is rewarded in happy Christian marriage. By way of contrast, *Dorido and Clorinia* presents the tragic destiny of two passion-ridden lovers who disregard religious precepts; this story derives its inspiration from medieval courtly literature. It is evident that the novelettes of Part I are set off against each other; the virtuous example of *Ozmín and Daraja* helps illuminate the pitfalls to be avoided in *Dorido and Clorinia.* The same symmetrical pattern is observed in the novelettes of Part II, but in reverse order: the protagonists of *Don Luis de Castro* will be chastised for their licentiousness, while the virtue of *Bonifacio and Dorotea* offers a model for emulation. Both stories of Part II are based on Italian *novelle.* The *novella* was not noted for its morality; therefore it may appear that Alemán chose for his point of departure a literary tradition ill suited to his exemplary purpose. But this preference for source material apparently antithetical to his intention is symptomatic of Alemán's state of mind—that of the Spanish Baroque, a period whose chief characteristic is the contradictory formula *Sic et Non* ("Yes and No").[2] Like the picaresque adventures of *Guzmán,* these novelettes display a tension between immoral adventures and religion, a paradoxical situation which allows the reader to savor the fillip of the sensual at the same time that he self-righteously censures in.

The novelettes of Part I underwent greater elaboration in Alemán's hands than those of Part II. The first two stories represent a blending of themes and motifs from many different sources, whereas the latter two are in large part adapted from a single model. *Ozmín and Daraja* and *Dorido and Clorinia* are certainly exceptions to Cervantes' claim in the prologue to his *Novelas ejemplares* (*Exemplary Novels*) to be the first Spaniard to write novelettes that were not translations of foreign works.

It is apparent that circumstances in Alemán's agitated life forced him to intercalate adaptations, rather than original stories, in Part II of *Guzmán*. Whereas Alemán had many years of leisure to compose the first half of his picaresque novel, he revised the second half hurriedly in order to reply to Juan Martí's apocryphal continuation. Had the author had more time to prepare his authentic second part, he likely would have composed stories similar to those of Part I. Alemán usually interpolates his novelettes at the end of one of the three books into which each part is divided. The fact that *Don Luis de Castro* does not follow this pattern indicates that it is a part of the revision of Part II; normally it would have come at the conclusion of Book I, instead of in the middle.

Mateo Alemán's novelettes have been so admired in Spain and abroad that they have had individual printings. Nor are imitations lacking. Thomas Porter's comedy, *The French Conjurer* (London, 1678) is based on *Dorido and Clorinia* and *Bonifacio and Dorotea*. (Porter completely changes the spirit of the novelettes, turning them into a ribald farce.) And Fletcher and Massinger appear to have received inspiration from *Don Luis de Castro* for Act III of their comedy, *The Little French Lawyer* (London, 1647).

II Ozmín and Daraja

Ozmín and Daraja (1599) is the last of three works that comprise the genre of the Moorish novel in Spain; the other two are *El Abencerraje y la hermosa Jarifa* (*The Abencerraje and the*

Beautiful Jarifa [1561]), of unknown authorship,[3] and the *Guerras civiles de Granada* (*Civil Wars of Granada* [1595-1619]), by Ginés Pérez de Hita. Alemán's initial inspiration was the first of these two, a short literary masterpiece that achieved great popularity immediately after its publication. *The Abencerraje* relates a charming love story placed in the exotic and romantic setting of Granada a few years before the fall of the Moslem kingdom in 1492. Its pages are adorned with oriental pageantry, acts of derring-do, and lofty examples of generosity, integrity, and virtue. *Ozmín and Daraja* has usually been regarded as a polished recasting of *The Abencerraje,* and therefore another picturesque idealization of the Moor of Granada. This is true only in part, however. The Baroque creative genius of Mateo Alemán was too complex to limit itself to such a modest and, in his concept, frivolous purpose. This was the writer who, several years later, wanted his picaresque novel to be remembered with the epithet of "The Watchtower on Human Life," rather than "The Rogue." *Ozmín and Daraja* has the same profundity of intention that characterizes *Guzmán de Alfarache.* There is much beneath its surface of romantic love between two beautiful and noble young Moors.

The plot of *Ozmín and Daraja is* as follows: During the siege of Baza in 1488-1489, the forces of the Catholic Monarchs capture the lovely Daraja, daughter of the Moorish governor of that city. Queen Isabella takes the girl into her retinue and treats her with the utmost kindness. When the Queen later goes to witness the besieging of Granada, she leaves Daraja in Seville, in the care of one of her favorites, Don Luis de Padilla. Daraja is engaged to Ozmín, a Moorish cavalier; they were going to be married when the war disrupted their plans. Ozmín falls ill when he learns that his fiancée has been taken prisoner, but he arises from his sickbed to journey to Seville in search of Daraja. Before arriving at that city, he falls into the hands of a Christian captain, but is able to buy his freedom with a bribe. To gain entrance into Don Luis' house, Ozmín adopts the name of Ambrosio and works first as a mason's helper and then as a gardener. Suspicions are aroused in the household when Daraja and Ambrosio are often seen conversing alone. Daraja allays these misgivings by affirming that the gardener is her betrothed's servant. Don

Rodrigo, the son of Don Luis, becomes enamored of Daraja and asks Ambrosio to aid him in gaining her good will. On seeing that the gardener does not support his wishes, Don Rodrigo has him dismissed. Ozmín retains his servant's clothes and goes to serve Don Alonso, who also is in love with Daraja. The Moorish girl becomes very sad without Ozmín; so, in order to entertain her, Don Luis prepares elaborate bullfights, mock battles with canes, and jousting tournaments. Ozmín disguises himself and triumphs in these games. Since Daraja continues to be depressed, Don Luis' family takes her to the country. Ozmín follows, together with Don Alonso, and the two gentlemen are attacked without provocation by the peasants of the village. In the fray Ozmín kills several peasants and wounds many more, but finally falls prisoner. In spite of the efforts of Don Alonso and Don Rodrigo, Ozmín is condemned to be hanged. Minutes before the execution, the Moor is saved by order of the King and Queen. The lovers are converted to Christianity and Ferdinand and Isabella are godfather and godmother at their wedding.

From this summary it is evident that the inspiration for the argument of *Ozmín and Daraja* is not to be sought in *The Abencerraje,* as has been thought, but rather in Classical literature. Once the Moorish trappings have been stripped away from *Ozmín and Daraja,* it becomes obvious that its basic plot follows very closely that of Heliodorus' *Ethiopian History.* In both Heliodorus and Alemán two faithful lovers who have decided to get married are repeatedly separated from one another by the caprices of Fate, but after many trials are finally united in marriage. The central motif of *Ozmín and Daraja* is precisely that of the Greek novel: the capture of the heroine by an enemy and the futile attempts of her suitor to recover her. The only difference is that Heliodorus develops the motif more extensively and introduces variations, such as the reversal of the lovers' roles.

In addition to these general similarities of plot, there are numerous other features common to both works. The protagonists, Ozmín and Daraja, are descendants of royal blood, like Theagenes and Chariclea, the Greek hero and heroine. The distinctive characteristic of Ozmín's and Daraja's love is its purity: the author describes their relations as a "most honest course of life" (*Rogue,* I, p. 67) and "chast and true love" (p. 97). This is in accord with the spirit of the *Ethiopian History,* where the dominant theme is chastity. Heliodorus describes the love of Theagenes and Chariclea as "a lawful feeling" (p. 25)[4] and "a pure and sober longing" (p. 151).

Alemán's Moorish lovers have the same attitude toward lying and deceit as their Greek predecessors. Chariclea believes that ". . . falsehood can be honourable when it assists the speaker without doing any real injury to the hearers" (p. 26), and the Greek lovers make up false life histories whenever they find themselves in a difficult situation (pp. 22-23, 174). Ozmín and Daraja are just as adept as Theagenes and Chariclea at fabricating plausible autobiographies to conceal their true identities (pp. 69, 74-75, 88-90, 95-96).

Like Chariclea (Books I-II, IV-V, VII-VIII, X), Daraja is virtually besieged by men of an enemy culture (all Spaniards in Daraja's case) who wish to marry her (p. 76). Don Rodrigo's and Don Alonso's requests that Ozmín act as go-between in their love affairs with Daraja (pp. 76-77, 80) are reworkings of the episode in which Chariclea is asked to persuade Theagenes to have sexual relations with Arsace, who is holding them both captive (pp. 181-82). The fit of jealousy that seizes Ozmín because of Don Rodrigo's pretensions to Daraja (pp. 77-78) echoes Theagenes' jealousy when Chariclea feigns to accept a pirate leader's proposal of marriage (pp. 24-26). Daraja falls sick from melancholy when she is separated from Ozmín for the second time and nobody can discover the cause of her ailment (pp. 81 ff.). This is similar to Chariclea's lovesickness which also confounds the physicians (pp. 75 ff.).

Ozmín triumphs in the bullfights and jousting tournament, while Daraja watches with a mixture of pride and anguish (pp. 82-91). This scene is reminiscent of Theagenes' victory in the footrace in the Pythian Games, which is likewise witnessed by his beloved (pp. 87-88). It may also be noted that in both books a splendid procession precedes the games. The incident of the loose bull that Ozmín kills (p. 85) recalls a similar episode in Heliodorus' novel, where Theagenes also displays his extraordinary strength and dexterity by overcoming a bull (pp. 267-69).

One of the most significant episodes of *Ozmín and Daraja* is that in which the hero makes no effort to defend himself when he is on trial for his life for having killed several peasants (pp. 99-100). This passivity would be inexplicable in a Moorish gallant of the lineage of the intrepid Abencerrajes, but is readily explainable as an element imitated from Ozmín's Greek predecessors, who likewise refuse to defend themselves when being tried for their lives (pp. 202-3, 267-76). When it appears that Ozmín is going to be executed, Daraja is tempted to take her own life (p. 97). Theagenes and Chariclea often contemplate suicide when they find themselves in similar situations (pp. 33, 35, 202-4).

The outcome of the Moorish novelette is clearly an imitation of the ending of the *Ethiopian History*. In both works the kings, like true *dei ex machina,* solve the lovers' problems by saving the heroes from death and by sponsoring their marriages. Both happy endings are brought about gratuitously after the protagonists have got into a situation from which they can not extricate themselves.

There are certain other details in *Ozmín and Daraja* which may also have been inspired by the *Ethiopian History*, but since they are commonplaces in Golden Age literature, they can not be considered *per se* as proof of Heliodorus' influence. For example, both the Greek and Moorish couples constantly refer to themselves as "husband and wife," although they are only engaged to be married. Ozmín's disguising himself in order to enter the house where Daraja is being held is akin to the episode in the *Ethiopian History* where Chariclea hides her nobility under a beggar's cloak and sets out to seek Theagenes (p. 152). Ozmín uses the trick of "deceiving with the truth" to foil a rival suitor of Daraja (p. 77); there are two instances of this same device in Heliodorus (pp. 25, 202). Finally, Alemán expounds ideas about beauty and nobility which are also found in Heliodorus' novel. Heliodorus, in the classical Greek tradition, identifies physical beauty with moral perfection (p. 162), and assumes that physical and moral beauty are present only in persons of noble birth (pp. 173, 273). Alemán likewise identifies beauty of body with beauty of soul (p. 66) and uses this criterion for distinguishing people of gentle birth (pp. 75, 87).

It is not surprising that Alemán was among the many Spanish imitators of Heliodorus. There existed great enthusiasm for the *Ethiopian History* at the University of Alcalá; since Alemán studied at this university, it was natural for him to share his professors' interest. It should also be noted that in 1596, three years before the appearance of *Ozmín and Daraja,* Alonso López Pinciano published his *Philosophía antigua poética,* in which he praised highly the *Ethiopian History,* comparing it with the *Iliad,* the *Odyssey,* and the *Aeneid.*

Although *Ozmín and Daraja* is a Moorish novel, it has only a few formal similarities in common with the other representatives of the genre. It coincides with *The Abencerraje* and the *Guerras civiles de Granada* in having Moorish protagonists with whom the author identifies himself; in the presentation of some picturesque facets of their Arabic civilization; and in the use of a historical frame that reproduces the struggle between Moors and Christians. Alemán also took a few minor details from *The Abencerraje* (the capture of Ozmín by a Christian captain, the garden scene in which the lovers are reunited, the fact that the protagonists have loved each other since childhood), and his descriptions of the bullfights, the mock combats, and the tournaments are inspired in the *Guerras civiles.* Like Pérez de Hita, Alemán has his Moors become Christians at the conclusion.

But *Ozmín and Daraja* lacks the most fundamental characteristic of the other novels: the idealization of the Moor. *The Abencerraje* came into being as a consequence of a new esteem for the Moors as a literary topic after the reconquest of Spain; its anonymous author gave novelistic form to the idealizations of the Moor found previously in ballads. The vision of the Moors presented in *The Abencerraje* corresponds to a purely literary and poetic idea of this vanquished people. The protagonists' nobleness and elevated sentiments give them an air of unreality analogous to that of the books of chivalry. Abindarráez of *The Abencerraje* is a model of knightly virtues: he is deeply in love, faithful and brave, and his word is as good as gold. His sweetheart Jarifa is beautiful, charming, and overcome with love for her gallant. In other words, they are Amadís and Oriana of the chivalresque *Amadís de Gaula* dressed as Moors, for their only genuinely Moorish characteristic is their gorgeous apparel. Even the historical personage, the Spaniard Rodrigo de Narváez, is bathed in the same poetically unreal light, instead of standing out sharply with his true attributes against the background of idealism that infuses the work. The Moors of Pérez de Hita's *Guerras civiles* are also prototypes of lofty gallantry and dashing chivalry.

Ozmín and Daraja offers a quite different view of the Moors; here the beautifully false idealizations of the Renaissance are absent. Ozmín and Daraja are of purely human stature; they are frail figures subject to the limitations and weaknesses of the ordinary human being. While the Moor Abindarráez of *The Abencerraje* always stays within the strictest limits of chivalry and enjoys the esteem and respect even of his enemies, who recognize him as an equal, Ozmín has recourse to such humiliating expedients as lying, and lowers himself to menial tasks. The Abencerraje can be proud of his race and his religion, but poor Ozmín must hide his inner sentiments and, denying his faith, pass himself off for something that he is not: a Christian. As for valor, Ozmín stands out in the games and tournaments, but does not realize truly superhuman exploits on the field of battle, as does Abindarráez. To gauge the enormous distance that separates the heroes, it suffices to compare an episode that Alemán adapted from *The Abencerraje* with the original: when Ozmín is going in search of his beloved, he is taken prisoner, as was the Abencerraje. But the circumstances of the capture are quite different. Abindarráez is finally overcome by Rodrigo de Narváez only after having vanquished five Christians, and his defeat is due in large part to fatigue. In contrast with this struggle of epic proportions sustained by the Abencerraje, Ozmín lets himself be arrested, together with his guide, without putting up the slightest resistance: "Now as soon as he [the Christian captain of the field] spied these two, he tooke hold of them" (*Rogue*, I, 69). This submissiveness denounces Ozmín's Greek ancestry: during Theagenes' peregrinations he is captured by one enemy after another, generally without attempting to defend himself. It is highly symptomatic that Alemán superimposes characteristics of the Greek novel on an episode borrowed from *The Abencerraje*. This detail demonstrates how the Baroque writer rejects Renaissance idealizations. The end of the incident illustrates well the contrast between the idealism characteristic of the Renaissance and the disenchantment of the Baroque. In *The Abencerraje* Rodrigo de Narváez is generous to the point of magnanimity with his captive: in exchange for a promise to return within three days, he allows the enamored Moor to carry out the clandestine visit that his sweetheart had granted him; later he arranges their marriage and overwhelms them with gifts. Christians and Moors compete to outdo each other in generosity. This high-mindedness contrasts sharply with the sordid self-interest portrayed in *Ozmín and Daraja*: it is obvious that Ozmín's captor is only looking for a bribe, and once his greed has been satisfied he releases the Moor without worrying about his duty to the King as a frontier guard. Apparently Ozmín's tribulations do not end here, for the narrator remarks with disillusionment: "Attended with these and other the like misfortunes, they arrived at length at *Sevill* . . ." (*Rogue*, I, 70). After comparing these two episodes, which are key passages for the appreciation of the different nuances of the Moorish novel, it is impossible to accept the Renaissance qualities of optimism and idealism as the outstanding characteristics of *Ozmín and Daraja*, as has been proposed.[5]

Further evidence of the essentially Renaissance nature of *The Abencerraje* and the Baroque quality of *Ozmín and Daraja* is supplied by their treatments of the religious theme. In *The Abencerraje* the spirit of chivalry and of tolerance precludes religious worries; the literary fondness for the Moors overlooks the difference in creed, barely alluding to it. On the other hand, one of the principal motifs in *Ozmín and Daraja* is the concern of the Christians for the salvation of the souls of the Moorish protagonists, since they take for granted that Christianity is the only true faith. Throughout the entire novelette, the Catholic Sovereigns express the hope that Daraja will be converted to Christianity. Don Rodrigo and Daraja's other Spanish suitors share the same desire, and it is clear that her conversion would be a prerequisite for a marriage with them (*Rogue*, I, 76-77). When their cities fall to the Christians, Ozmín's and Daraja's parents ask to be baptized, as though they suddenly become aware of the error of their belief. When Ozmín is on his way to the gallows, the people of Seville exhort him to confess and "not lose body and soule both at once" (p. 100).[6] Through the whole work the theme of the redemption of the lovers runs parallel to the theme of their efforts to be reunited; these two threads are drawn together in the denouement, in the presence of the King and Queen. The attempts of the Christians to proselytize Ozmín and Daraja are as persistent as the endeavors of the Moors to come together. At the end the Monarchs save Ozmín's life, and God, through His grace, saves both his and Daraja's souls, bringing them to "the knowledge of his truth . . ." (p. 101). Considering the importance of the religious theme in *Ozmín and Daraja*,[7] it is logical that Alemán, imitating the ending of the *Ethiopian History*, should utilize the technique of the *deus ex machina* to solve the protagonists' dilemma. The intervention of the Catholic (an especially appropriate epithet) Sovereigns to save the Moors' bodies is a reflection of the divine intervention to save their souls.

It is apparent that *Ozmín and Daraja* does not have a single unified theme, as do its models, the Greek novel and the Moorish novel. There is rather a bipartite theme: the reunion of the lovers (the mundane theme) and their union with God (the religious theme). This is the same basic duality found in *Guzmán de Alfarache*: on the one hand, the partiality for adventure; on the other, the preoccupation with the welfare of the protagonist's soul. There is also a parallel in the structure of the two works. In *Guzmán* the protagonist faces a long series of adventures, which give the narrator the opportunity to make moralistic reflections and to interpolate misanthropic digressions. Alemán's procedure is to present an evil act in the plot and then to comment on it. The novelist employs the same technique in *Ozmín and Daraja*. Throughout the story appear examples of human wickedness, followed by the appropriate moralistic meditations: the venality of the captain who seeks a bribe (*Rogue*, I, 69); the distrust and morbid curiosity that exists everywhere toward strangers (p. 70); the envy that Ozmín's working companions feel toward him (p. 70); the gossip about Daraja's relations with the gardener (pp. 72-73); the impunity with which nobles can commit outrages (p. 81); the hypocrisy present in social relations (p. 81); and the hate that persons of base estate feel toward their superiors (pp. 94-96).[8] The resulting complex structure, typical of the Baroque, contrasts greatly with the Renaissance simplicity of *The Abencerraje.* As for ideological content, the disparity between the disillusionment that frequently comes to the surface in *Ozmín and Daraja* and the optimistic joy that pervades *The Abencerraje* offers an interesting comparison of the treatment of the same subject by a writer of the Renaissance and another of the Baroque.

Ozmín and Daraja is not cut from the same piece of cloth as *The Abencerraje* and the *Guerras civiles de Granada.* While the content of these last two novels is limited to an idealized vision of the Grenadine Moor, Alemán's novelette has a more profound and edifying purpose (although it is equally superficial in its treatment of the Moor and his culture). It presents the story of two Moorish sweethearts who, like the hero and heroine of the Greek novel, face successive reversals of fortune in a vain attempt to be reunited; these sufferings have a divine intention, for in this way God has seen fit to bring the lovers to a knowledge of the one and only true religion.

Contrary to what has often been affirmed, *Ozmín and Daraja* is far from being an interlude of optimism and idealism (characteristics of the Renaissance) interpolated in a novel that contains somber and pessimistic passages (Baroque). The same sentiments of pessimism and disillusionment found in the body of *Guzmán de Alfarache* also appear in abbreviated form in *Ozmín and Daraja.* Alemán's Moorish novelette is an optimistic work insofar as virtue triumphs at the end. But this happy conclusion is a sugar-coated pill, for alongside the fulfillment of the mundane desires (the marriage of the Moorish couple) is included the moral lesson (their conversion to Christianity). The appeal of Mateo Alemán to his age is precisely this: He knows how to delight the reader with the narration of entertaining adventures at the same time that he teaches him moral lessons. In *Guzmán* the moral teachings are to be gleaned from the picaresque adventures; in *Ozmín and Daraja* they are intermingled with the wanderings of the two faithful lovers and with the descriptions of bullfights, mock battles, and jousts. Skillful writer that he is, Alemán exploits three popular types of the novel—the picaresque, the Moorish, and the Greek—but always adapting them to his own artistic purposes. The creator of *The*

Rogue demonstrates his virtuosity when he combines the Moorish novel and the Greek novel in *Ozmín and Daraja.* By thus fusing literary genres Alemán is a worthy precursor of Cervantes.

III Dorido and Clorinia

In *Ozmín and Daraja,* as was seen, Alemán defends the licit quality of love. The Moors' passion is chaste and noble, and ultimately finds just guerdon in Christian marriage. In contrast, *Dorido and Clorinia* owes its inspiration to the medieval tradition of courtly love which found true love outside matrimony. Medieval stories did not end in marriage, and often presented adulterous relationships. Since illicit love was a sin worthy of death, tragic endings were obligatory for Tristan and Iseult, Lancelot and Guenevere, Fiammetta and Panfilo. Fifteenth century Spanish literature followed the European tradition of ill-fated lovers: the most notable examples are the sentimental novel, such as San Pedro's *Cárcel de amor* (*Prison of Love*) and *La Celestina.* Most Spanish works avoid the theme of adultery, but preserve the denouement of moralistic overtone; such is Alemán's story.

Dorido and Clorinia is a tale of love, cruel murder, and revenge involving the young lovers named in the story's title. The plot and setting are Italianate. The lovers converse at night through a hole in the wall of Clorinia's house. Oracio, an intimate friend of Dorido's, also conceives a passion for Clorinia. He wishes to marry her, and knowing that Dorido has no such intention, he asks Dorido to cede Clorinia to him. This Dorido agrees to do. But Clorinia loves only Dorido and will not have Oracio. The lovers continue seeing each other. One night the jealous Oracio goes to the hole before Dorido, takes Clorinia's hand, and severs it with a knife. Clorinia is on the point of death; her family despairs. Dorido decides to avenge his mistress. In order to have the right to do so, he marries Clorinia secretly. A few days later he invites Oracio to supper, drugs him, cuts off both his hands, and strangles him. Dorido then conveys the body to the scene of the crime and hangs it in the hole. He places a sonnet around Oracio's neck, telling of his treachery. Clorinia dies later that day and Dorido flees.

It will be noted that Alemán uses no *deus ex machina* to produce the inevitable tragic ending of the passion-consumed lovers; the presence of a rival suitor provides a convincing motivation. A hundred years earlier, Diego de San Pedro had used the same device to bring to an unhappy conclusion both of his sentimental novels, *Arnalte y Lucenda* and *Cárcel de amor*.

Alemán's tale differs from the typical story of courtly tradition, which only treats illicit or unapproved love that ends tragically. To the themes of unsanctioned love and its disastrous conclusion, *Dorido and Clorinia* adds that of revenge. The addition of the element of vengeance gives a different turn to the story, for it modifies the usual medieval connotations of supernatural retribution. The punishment of the lovers still appears to be of divine origin, but the victims are able to strike back at the human instrument of God's wrath (this is also true of the novels of San Pedro).

The theme of violent reprisal is typical of the Italian *novelle*, particularly of those of Matteo Bandello. This has led critics to conjecture that Alemán took his story from an Italian model; however, no direct source has been discovered. It seems more likely that the story is original, although Alemán drew upon a wide variety of sources for its conception and elaboration. In *Dorido and Clorinia* there are reminiscences of Classical mythology, the literature of courtly love, and the Italian *novella*. The product of this combination of themes and motifs from disparate sources is a work of originality.

As already noted, the principal outline of *Dorido and Clorinia* is based on the medieval tradition of the ill-starred lovers who do not seek religious sanction for their passion and consequently suffer a tragic fate. As in *La Celestina* and many Italian *novelle*, there is no obstacle preventing the protagonists from consecrating their love in marriage; it is simply not their wish. The description of their first interview makes clear that their attraction to each other is physical in nature:

> *Dorido* intreated her hand, and she willingly gave it him; he tooke it, and kist it againe and againe . . . stroking his face therewith, never suffering it to depart from his mouth. After . . . he stretched forth his

[hand] to her . . . countenance, unable to enjoy any other pleasure, nor could that place and time affoord him any farther content. (*Rogue*, I, 258)

Treated by a severe moralist like Mateo Alemán, such an affair can end only in disaster. There are other traces of the courtly tradition in this "exemplary novel." The secrecy with which Dorido surrounds his relations with Clorinia (I, 256, 258-60) is one of the tenets of what came to be called *amour courtois* ("courtly love"). When Dorido intercedes for Oracio with his own lady, he tells Clorinia that she should give Oracio the *bel accueil* ("fond reception"), even if she feels no love for him (I, 261). The fact that Clorinia does not cry out when Oracio is severing her hand is probably a reflection of the exaggerated sense of honor typical of courtly love; she prefers death to letting her love affair become known.

Alemán's other borrowings consist of motifs, rather than themes. A good example is the lovers' communication through a hole in the wall—an obvious derivation of the myth of Pyramus and Thisbe. In order to converse with his lady, Dorido scales a wall facing the hole; this detail is apparently taken from Jorge de Montemayor's *Diana* (Clásicos Castellanos ed. [Madrid, 1954], p. 157). The motif of the gallant who gives up his beloved to a friend is found in a tale that achieved extraordinary popularity in European literature and folklore—the story of the two friends.[9] Alemán was doubtless acquainted with several of the many versions of this story in Latin, Italian, and Spanish literature; however, he utilized only the self-sacrifice motif, a small portion of the original story. The picaresque novelist manifests his pessimistic view of humanity in the other motif that he intertwines with Dorido's self-renunciation: that of the treacherous friend. Instead of repaying Dorido's selfless action with another sacrifice, as in the story of the two friends, Oracio returns evil for good, mutilating his friend's sweetheart (again it is noteworthy that the treacherous friend motif appears in both of San Pedro's novels). Oracio approaches Clorinia by imitating her lover's dress and voice—a common situation in the *novella* (and a frequent dramatic device in the Golden Age theater).

Another typically Italian motif is the severing of hands as a punishment for amorous offenses. In Alemán's time, amputation of one or more limbs was a current punishment for crime in Europe. However, as a private method of revenge for crimes of love, mutilation is peculiar to the Italian *novella.* Offended lovers or husbands who avenge themselves by mutilation are particularly abundant in Bandello.[10] However, Alemán introduced a change in the use of the motif: in Bandello the amputation of limbs was a punishment for infidelity, while Oracio is merely a rejected admirer. No direct literary precedent is known for the sonnet that Dorido attaches to the neck of his dead rival, telling of his treacherous conduct toward Clorinia. This device was possibly inspired by Bandello's frequent use of the sonnet engraved on star-crossed lovers' tombs, relating their misfortunes.[11]

In *Dorido and Clorinia* Mateo Alemán not only weaves familiar motifs into an original pattern, but also transforms the motifs. Alemán's creative process—the molding of new tales from old themes and motifs—was characteristic of the Italian master storytellers. The result is an uncommon *novella,* full of horror and pathos, and comparable to the best of Boccaccio and Bandello.

IV Don Luis de Castro

Critics of *Guzmán de Alfarache* up to now have been generally agreed that the story of *Don Luis de Castro and Don Rodrigo de Montalvo* is merely a translation of Masuccio Salernitano's forty-first tale. As often happens, scholars have perpetuated a careless judgment without evaluating it. The fact is that Alemán preserved intact only the kernel of his model—the central situation that differentiates this story from hundreds of other *novelle* of amorous theme. He modified most of the supporting narration in both form and content. Alemán's changes include a different narrative point of view, a new introduction, the grafting of another tale upon the original story, and a different ending, in addition to the usual alterations of names, nationalities, historical setting, and scene of action. It is therefore apparent that Alemán's version contains about as many differences from Masuccio's tale as similarities to it.

Not all the Spanish novelist's changes are original: a story from the *Decameron* was instrumental in the conception of *Don Luis de Castro* (see below). However, as with Masuccio's story, Alemán systematically modified the material he imitated from Boccaccio. Alemán's innovations are just as significant as his borrowings, for, as will be seen, they reflect a different attitude toward life—the attitude of the Spanish Baroque, so distinct from that of the Italian Renaissance.

The action of Masuccio's story is as follows: Filippo and Ciarlo, French cavaliers in the army of Duke Ranier of Anjou, are in love with two Florentine sisters. Before they can arrange a nocturnal meeting, the gallants must return to France, and soon forget their mistresses. In order to revive Filippo's passion, his lady sends him a counterfeit ring with the inscription "False diamond, why hast thou forsaken me?" Filippo and Ciarlo return to Florence.

On arrival, Filippo receives an assignation with his mistress, but Ciarlo must go to bed with the lady's husband so he will not miss her should he awake. Ciarlo passes a most fearful night. Toward daybreak Filippo and his lady burst joyously into Ciarlo's room and inform him that his bedfellow was his sweetheart, not the husband. To set right the fault, the lovers again divide into pairs; Filippo and Ciarlo disport themselves with their mistresses until the husband returns from a trip.

It is evident that Masuccio's story has two sections or episodes. The first serves as an introduction to the second, and at the same time constitutes an independent narrative. The introductory subplot presents the characters of the primary action and establishes their amorous relationship. But this forepart also stands by itself, because it has a climactic action: by means of an ingenious device (the counterfeit ring), Filippo's lady achieves the return of her unfaithful lover. Another peculiarity of the preliminary section is that the masculine protagonists serve a historical personage, Duke Ranier of Anjou.

Mateo Alemán retains the composite structure of Masuccio's tale, and attaches to it a separate introduction. *Don Luis de Castro* starts with a frame story: Don Alvaro de Luna, the renowned Constable of Castile, offers a diamond ring to Don Luis or Don Rodrigo, as a reward for the better of two love stories to be told by them. It will be noticed that Alemán has transferred to the frame two elements from Masuccio's introductory episode: the historical figure and the diamond ring. However, following his usual procedure, the picaresque novelist transforms the borrowed material. Alvaro de Luna clearly corresponds to Duke Ranier, but he plays a much more important part (Ranier does not even appear in the action of Masuccio's story). Alemán also assigns a different function to the ring, connecting it to the historical character. In doing so, Alemán interweaves his model's motif of the ring with a different novelistic tradition, that of the patron who stimulates reciters of tales with a prize. At the end, the Constable does not award the ring to either storyteller, but to the girl who spent the night with Don Rodrigo. Alemán's frame technique necessitates a shift from Masuccio's omniscient point of view to the first-person narration of Don Luis and Don Rodrigo. However, continuity is achieved by making Don Rodrigo's tale a sequel to Don Luis', and by having both raconteurs figure as protagonists in the central episode.

For his principal narrative, Alemán follows Masuccio's technique of joining two independent stories into one. He also subordinates the first tale to the second, making the preliminary story set the stage for the more novel happenings of the main plot. However, the Spanish novelist does not imitate the content of Masuccio's introductory tale. This is to be expected, since he had already used the diamond motif in his frame. In Alemán's preliminary tale, Don Luis de Castro complains that for many years he served a certain great lady with all secrecy and gallantry, spending his entire inheritance on the courtship; but when his fortune was exhausted, his lady married another. Boccaccio furnished the inspiration for this story: in the *Decameron* V, 9, Federigo degli Alberighi also squanders his patrimony in unrequited love.

Don Rodrigo's tale—the center of interest—is a continuation of the love story of Don Luis. The latter receives the fulfillment of his desires from his mistress, while Don Rodrigo accompanies her husband. This part of Alemán's novelette follows Masuccio closely. But the denouement is wholly different: whereas in the Italian version Ciarlo finally enjoys his lady, Don Rodrigo is so put to shame that he can only slink away to recover his clothes and depart. Alemán's ending has none of the sensuous joy of living and the exuberant immorality of his Italian model; rather it echoes the somber overtones of *Guzmán de Alfarache*, where the protagonist's amorous adventures inevitably fail, leaving him the butt of raillery. Thus Alemán transforms a Renaissance story of almost pagan exaltation of sensuality into a typical product of the Spanish Baroque—bitter disillusionment with worldly pleasures. Eros has come under the scrutiny of Alemán's "Watch-tower on Human Life" and has been banished.

In view of the ending of Don Rodrigo's tale, it is easy to understand why Alemán changed Masuccio's introductory story. The Italian novelist was preparing a happy ending for his cavaliers—hence the optimistic and carefree mood of the preliminary tale. Since Alemán's story was to conclude in mockery for Don Rodrigo and a hollow victory for Don Luis, it was appropriate that his introductory story also close on a pessimistic note. At first glance, it might appear that Don Luis triumphs at the end, since he receives his mistress' favors. Such is not the case, however. Don Luis' intention was to marry his lady, not merely to have an adventure with her, as was Federigo's purpose in the *Decameron*. However, Federigo was ultimately rewarded with his lady's hand, while Don Luis simply gained an amorous interview in return for his inheritance and years of faithful service. Don Luis obviously considers himself a loser in his amorous enterprise, for he refers to it as a great misfortune. The distance between Italian Renaissance optimism and Spanish Baroque pessimism is manifest in the fact that Boccaccio's gallant gets more than he could have hoped for, whereas Alemán's lover must accept a fleeting moment of pleasure in place of the lifetime of contentment and well-being he desired. The Spanish novelist has turned Boccaccio's conclusion inside out.

In Alemán's introductory tale, Don Luis sees his hopes of marriage turn to ashes; in the central episode Don Rodrigo is made an object of scorn while performing a favor for a friend. At the end of the frame story, both become double losers, seeing the promised diamond slip through their fingers—a fitting ending for a recital of Baroque disenchantment.

V Bonifacio and Dorotea

The source of Alemán's last novelette, *Bonifacio and Dorotea,* is Masuccio's thirty-second tale.[12] This story deals with a favorite theme of the Italian Renaissance novel—the cuckolding of an unsuspecting husband. A Florentine is enamored of Iustina, the virtuous wife of a goldbeater. To overcome her chastity, the astute gallant has an old servant feign to be in the service of an abbess and buy gold thread from Iustina's husband. After gaining the couple's confidence, the old woman persuades Iustina to spend two or three days with the abbess. On the appointed day, several apparently respectable ladies pass by for Iustina and continue toward the convent. Actually, these women are in the employ of the Florentine, and they leave Iustina at his house. Seeing that resistance would be in vain, Iustina has a pleasant supper with her seducer and accedes to his desires. During the night fire breaks out and a captain of the watch—who happens to be an admirer of Iustina—breaks in the doors to lend aid. Upon seeing Iustina with the Florentine, the captain's love changes into fierce hatred. He throws Iustina into prison, with the intention of publicly disgracing her the following day. However, the Florentine has the old servant go to the jail, exchange clothes with Iustina, and remain in her place. When the prisoner is taken before the judges, all believe that the captain's passion has blinded him. Iustina returns to her husband, who never suspects what has happened.

In *Bonifacio and Dorotea* Alemán followed his source more closely than in any other novelette, but the impression his story leaves is totally different from that of Masuccio. The astonishing thing is that Alemán introduced few modifications in form, and yet changed completely the spirit of the tale. Alemán's alterations consist largely of shifts of emphasis, rather than the introduction of new elements. In Masuccio's tale, interest revolves around the Florentine's ingenious scheme for seducing Iustina and his astuteness in extricating himself from the ensuing predicament. He is the mastermind who plans all the moves his old servant makes to ensnare the victim. Masuccio's conclusion is both a tribute to the Florentine's cleverness and a rejoicing in his success.

Alemán shifts the center of interest from the seducer to the victim and her husband, as is denoted by the title of *Bonifacio and Dorotea.* To make Dorotea more important, Alemán has to diminish interest in the seducer (Claudio). Thus he transfers the Florentine's ingeniousness to the go-between; the increased importance of this figure is reflected in the fact that Alemán gives her a name (Sabina), while Masuccio's old woman remained anonymous. Spanish literature offered an illustrious model for such bawds—Celestina. It is therefore not surprising that Sabina is a sorceress, as well as a procuress: "She was . . . so curious in visiting Church-yards, so charitable in accompanying those that were to be hang'd, that shee was able to make water-cresses to grow on the top of a bed" (*Rogue,* II, 200). But in order not to imitate too closely Fernando de Rojas' creation, Alemán makes Sabina an attractive young slave, instead of an ugly old hag.

Having stripped Claudio of his predecessor's ingenuity, Alemán makes of his villain a pale figure. Unlike the Florentine (and like Calisto of the *Celestina*), Claudio arrives at no solution for possessing Dorotea—it is Sabina who contrives all and fulfills her master's desires with her arts. Claudio's importance is so limited that he is imprisoned by the captain of the watch at the same time as Dorotea. Sabina then devises the trick of taking Dorotea's place in jail.

Since Dorotea is the central figure in Alemán's novelette, her character is sketched in with many more details than in Masuccio's version. Much space is devoted to her family, her upbringing, and her courtship and married life with Bonifacio. All this background information points up her virtue, which is much more deep-seated than Iustina's. Whereas the latter "acted with due discretion and made a virtue of necessity," and "supped in jovial wise with the Florentine,"[13] surrendering almost willingly to his wishes, Dorotea holds off Claudio as long as is humanly possible:

> Shee defended her selfe . . . as well as shee could . . . when shee saw that she could no longer hold out against him . . . shee yeelded up the Fort unto him, for want of succours . . . she a lone-woman; he strong, and she weake; and none can do more than they can doe. (*Rogue,* II, 205)[14]

The problem examined by Alemán is Dorotea's honor—a subject Masuccio passed over with only an ironic allusion to the female members of his audience. After the rape, when she is again safely home, Dorotea faces the dilemma of whether or not to tell Bonifacio of her dishonor. However, contrary to the practice of the contemporary drama, there is no soul-searching; the author simply states that "*Dorotea* remayned with her husband in the same peace and love as before . . ." (II, 208). Dorotea decides that the wisest course is to maintain silence; nothing is to be gained by committing suicide or by demanding vengeance by her husband. Alemán's avoidance of these latter solutions is important, for it demonstrates his attitude toward honor. The tradition of Lucretia was common in contemporary literature; however, it was no more than a literary solution—beautiful in theory, but of no relevance as an example of conduct, for it led to damnation of the soul. And if Dorotea had incited Bonifacio to take revenge on Claudio, she would have run the risk of putting her husband's life in danger, and in any case, he would be unnecessarily saddened on learning of her calamity. Since Dorotea is not at fault, she has nothing to be ashamed of. Moreover, circumstances favor the virtuous wife. According to the code widely accepted in Golden Age literature, honor depended on appearances more than on realities; if an affront remained unknown, there was no loss of honor as far as society was concerned.[15] Alemán stresses that Bonifacio's honor remains intact, because "*Sabina*, and most of them that knew the affront that was done him, dyed within a few dayes after" (II, 208).

The world of Mateo Alemán's novelettes is a Utopian one in which virtue is rewarded and evil is punished. Therefore the ending of Masuccio's tale had to be altered, to chasten the violator. Alemán metes out punishment according to the long-practiced *lex talionis* ("law of retaliation"): when Claudio is released from prison, he is struck dumb by the news that his sister had been found in bed with a servant, smothered by the fire. His dishonor is notorious throughout the city. The sweet morsel turns to bitter gall in Claudio's mouth; his triumph was momentary, and his infamy eternal. The seducer is affected so profoundly that he follows the medieval tradition of becoming a monk and doing penance in the desert. Alemán concludes:

"So just is God in all his workes, and so well doth he know how to punish those wrongs, that are offered to the innocent" (II, 208).

At the end of *Bonifacio and Dorotea* iniquity has been overcome and society has returned to normalcy. It may seem surprising that Alemán should have chosen such a violent subject for an exemplary novelette. However, his choice is readily explainable when placed in relation with the other intercalated tales. In his previous treatments, Alemán had dealt with pure love (*Ozmín and Daraja*), courtly love (*Dorido and Clorinia*), and adulterous love (*Don Luis de Castro*). These stories exemplified the three levels recognized by Renaissance theories of love: *amor purus* (nonsensual, hearts and minds only), *amor mixtus* (hearts and bodies), and *amor ferino* (purely sensual).[16] In the downward progression of his analysis of love in all its manifestations, only the rape, the last step of *amor ferino*, was lacking. In *Bonifacio and Dorotea* Alemán studies the social problems brought up by the violation of a chaste woman. His commonsense solution of the honor question is the same that Cervantes was to expound later in his exemplary novel *La fuerza de la sangre* (*The Force of Blood*). Both novelists played down the dramatic possibilities inherent in the situation and directed their attention to finding a realistic solution to problems vitally connected with life.

Notes and References

Chapter One

1. Except when otherwise stated, the present biography is based on Francisco Rodríguez Marín's fundamental studies, *Discursos leídos ante la Real Academia Española* . . . 2nd ed. (Sevilla: Francisco de P. Díaz, 1907), and *Documentos referentes a Mateo Alemán y a sus deudos más cercanos* (*1546-1607*) (Madrid: Archivos, 1933).

2. Alonso de Barros, in his laudatory prologue to Part I of *Guzmán*.

3. The reference is to Part II, Book iii, Chapter 4. Throughout this study "Part" and "Book" will be capitalized when they refer to *Guzmán*, in order to avoid confusion with their use in a generic sense.

4. See the numerous references under *médico* in Malcolm Jerome Gray's *An Index to "Guzmán de Alfarache"* (New Brunswick: Rutgers University Press, 1948).

5. Rodríguez Marín, *Discursos*, p. 19.

6. Joaquín Saura Falomir, Introduction, ed. of *Guzmán* (Madrid: Ediciones Castilla, 1953), I, p. 11.

7. The novelist reiterated his claim of pure Christian lineage in his second application to emigrate, that of 1607. He also alleged this by implication in a spurious coat of arms that he designed to accompany his portrait in his books; see Rodríguez Marín, *Documentos*, p. 54, note 1.

8. See Miguel Maticorena Estrada, "Nuevos datos sobre Mateo Alemán," *Estudios Americanos*, XX, No. 103 (1960), p. 60.

9. Claudio Guillén, "Los pleitos extremeños de Mateo Alemán: I. El juez, 'Dios de la tierra'," *Archivo Hispalense*, XXXII (1960), pp. 387-407, the principal basis for this Section VI.

10. Such duality was part of the Baroque ideology in seventeenth century Spain: rigid religious orthodoxy was insisted upon at the same time that moral laxity was tolerated. On the Baroque, see Chapter 2, note 5 below.

11. Germán Bleiberg, "Mateo Alemán y los galeotes," *Revista de Occidente*, año IV, 2ª época, no. 39 (1966), pp. 330-63, on which the present section is based.

12. This is apparent from the fact that the royal permission for publication bears the date of January 13, 1598. This permission is reproduced by R. Foulché-Delbosc, "Bibliographie de Mateo Alemán. 1598-1615," *Revue Hispanique,* XLII (1918), p. 488.

13. See Ludwig Pfandl, *Cultura y costumbres del pueblo español de los siglos XVI y XVII; introducción al estudio del Siglo de Oro* (Barcelona: Editorial Araluce, 1929), Chapter IX; and Agustín G. de Amezúa y Mayo, "Cómo se hacía un libro en nuestro Siglo de Oro," in *Opúsculos histórico-literarios,* I (Madrid: C. S. I. C., 1951), pp. 331-73.

14. Foulché-Delbosc (cited in note 12 above), p. 488.

15. See José Simón-Díaz, *Bibliografía de la literatura hispánica,* V (Madrid: C. S. I. C., 1958), pp. 127-33.

16. Later in the seventeenth century renditions were made into English (1622-1623), Latin (1652), and Dutch (1655). As late as the nineteenth century there were new translations: in Hungarian (1822-1824) and Portuguese (1848).

17. Those of Madrid: Várez de Castro, 1599; Madrid: Herederos de Juan Yñiguez de Lequerica, 1600; and Sevilla: Juan de León, 1602. These authentic editions contain a portrait of Alemán; see Foulché-Delbosc, pp. 550-52.

18. Luis de Valdés furnishes this information about Alemán's popularity in his eulogistic prologue to Part II of *Guzmán.*

19. *Agudeza y arte de ingenio* (*Acuteness and Art of Wit* [Huesca, 1648]), LVI. Some scholars have misinterpreted this passage, construing it to mean that Gracián casts doubt on Alemán's authorship of *Guzmán.* For example, see E. Correa Calderón, ed. of Gracián's *Obras completas* (Madrid: Aguilar, 1944), p. 259, note 1.

20. See Irving A. Leonard, "*Guzmán de Alfarache* in the Lima Book Trade, 1613," *Hispanic Review,* XI (1943), p. 213.

21. See Cristóbal Pérez Pastor, *Bibliografía madrileña,* II (Madrid: Archivos, 1906), p. 2; and Rodríguez Marín, *Documentos,* p. 38.

22. See Rodríguez Marín, *Documentos,* p. 42, and José Gestoso y Pérez, *Nuevos datos para ilustrar las biografías del Maestro Juan de Malara y de Mateo Alemán* (Sevilla: La Región, 1896), pp. 21-22.

23. The description is contained in Alemán's second application to emigrate; see Gestoso y Pérez, p. 21.

24. Margarita subsequently avowed that her mother's name was María de Espinosa (see Josefina Muriel, *Conventos de monjas en la Nueva España* [México: Editorial Santiago, 1946], p. 396); however, this may have been an attempt to allege legitimate birth, by adopting the surname of Alemán's wife. Another possibility is that the novelist had another lover named María de Espinosa.

25. See Rodríguez Marín, *Documentos,* pp. 34-35.

26. This is suggested by the circumstance that all the editions except the first were published outside of the kingdom of Valencia, the only area covered by Martí's copyright. For descriptions of the editions of the spurious *Guzmán,* see Foulché-Delbosc (cited in note 12 above) and Simón-Díaz (cited in note 15 above).

27. In his *Discursos,* p. 31, Rodríguez Marín conjectures that Rosso was out of town at the time of Alemán's imprisonment and that he immediately paid for the writer's release upon returning to Seville. But in his *Documentos,* p. 34, this same scholar publishes proof that Rosso was in Seville on December 30, 1602, and January 21, 1603.

28. This notarial document is reproduced by Luis Astrana Marín, *Vida ejemplar y heroica de Miguel de Cervantes Saavedra,* V (Madrid: Reus, 1953), pp. 344-45. For fuller details about the piracy and its printers, see my article, "A Pirated Edition of *Guzmán de Alfarache*: More Light on Mateo Alemán's Life," *Hispanic Review,* XXXIV (1966), pp. 326-28.

29. Rodríguez Marín, *Discursos,* pp. 33-34.

30. *Ibid.,* p. 34.

31. Rodríguez Marín, *Documentos,* pp. 48-49.

32. See Irving A. Leonard, "Mateo Alemán in Mexico: A Document," *Hispanic Review,* XVII (1949), p. 319. Leonard's study is one of the most valuable on Alemán's life.

33. See Julio Caro Baroja, *Los judíos en la España moderna y contemporánea* (Madrid: Ediciones Arión, 1962), II, pp. 335-43.

34. Rodríguez Marín, *Discursos,* p. 37.

35. See Alice H. Bushee, "The *Sucesos* of Mateo Alemán," *Revue Hispanique,* XXV (1911), pp. 422-23.

36. The unconventional spelling of *Guerra* reflects some of the orthographic doctrines that Alemán set forth in his *Ortografía castellana.*

37. See Pedro Henríquez Ureña, "Escritores españoles en la Universidad de México," *Revista de Filología Española,* XXII (1935), p. 62.

38. See Irving A. Leonard's article cited in note 32 above, pp. 324-30.

39. See José Toribio Medina, *La imprenta en México (1539-1821),* II (Santiago de Chile: Impreso en casa del autor, 1909), p. 43. Medina does not cite the source of his information.

40. See Muriel, *Conventos* (cited in note 24), pp. 367, 387, 396; and Dorothy Schons, *Notes from Spanish Archives,* I (Austin, Texas [Ann Arbor, Michigan]: Edwards Brothers, 1946), preface and p. 7.

41. See my article, "Was Mateo Alemán in Italy?" *Hispanic Review,* XXXI (1963), pp. 148-49, and the bibliography there cited.

42. For an excellent bibliographical orientation on the praise of

cities, see Joseph E. Gillet and Otis H. Green, *Propalladia and Other Works of Bartolomé de Torres Naharro,* IV (Philadelphia: University of Pennsylvania Press, 1961), pp. 281-85.

43. Paul Groussac, *Une Enigme littéraire* (Paris: A. Picard et fils, 1903), uncautiously conjectured that the same writer penned the apocryphal continuations of *Guzmán* and *Don Quixote.* Later it was discovered that Juan Martí, the author of the spurious *Guzmán,* died in 1604—ten years before the publication of the apocryphal *Quixote.*

44. Rodríguez Marín, *Discursos,* pp. 30-31, espoused the theory of the enmity between the novelists and hinted that he planned to point out spiteful allusions to Cervantes in *Guzmán.* However, it appears that he never published such a study. Urban Cronan's attempts ("Mateo Alemán and Miguel de Cervantes Saavedra," *Revue Hispanique,* XXV [1911], pp. 468-75) to find allusions to Cervantes in *Guzmán* are completely unconvincing.

Chapter Two

1. A few scholars prefer to consider *Lazarillo* a precursor of the genre, which would start with *Guzmán*; see Miguel Herrero (cited in note 10 below); Américo Castro, "El *Lazarillo de Tormes,*" in *Hacia Cervantes,* 2nd ed. (Madrid: Taurus, 1960), p. 135; M. Bataillon, Introduction, *La Vie de Lazarillo de Tormès* (Paris: Aubier, 1958), pp. 75-82; Fernando Lázaro Carreter, *Tres historias de España. Lazarillo de Tormes, Guzmán de Alfarache y Pablos de Segovia* (Salamanca: Universidad de Salamanca, 1960), pp. 19-20. This distinction between precursor and initiator of the genre has not been generally accepted, because all the essential characteristics of the picaresque novel are satisfied in, and indeed established by, *Lazarillo.* In another essay in *Hacia Cervantes,* Américo Castro specifically calls *Lazarillo* the first picaresque novel and Lázaro the first pícaro ("Perspectiva de la novela picaresca," pp. 112, 116, 119-21).

2. The present explanation is based on Claudio Guillén's valuable study, "Toward a Definition of the Picaresque," in *Proceedings of the IIIrd Congress of the International Comparative Literature Association* (The Hague: Mouton & Co., 1962), pp. 252-66.

3. See Franz Rauhut, "Influencia de la picaresca española en la literatura alemana," *Revista de Filología Hispánica,* I (1939), pp. 237-56.

4. On the French, English, and American derivations of the picaresque genre, see Robert Alter, *Rogue's Progress* (Cambridge, Mass.: Harvard University Press, 1964).

5. This bipolarity of thinking is typical of the seventeenth century Spanish Baroque, which is best described by the formula *Sic et Non*

("Yes and No"); see Otis H. Green, *Spain and the Western Tradition,* I (Madison: University of Wisconsin Press, 1963), p. 207. The same kind of "truancy," or temporary departure from accepted moral codes in order to have fun, is found in the fourteenth century Spanish masterpiece, *Libro de buen amor* (*Book of Good Love*) by Juan Ruiz; see Green, *Spain,* I, Chapter II. This similarity of spirit points up the affinity of the Baroque with the Middle Ages in Spain. Both *Guzmán* and the *Libro de buen amor* are pseudo-autobiographies.

It should be pointed out here that no universally accepted definition of the Baroque has yet been devised; see René Wellek, "The Concept of Baroque in Literary Scholarship," in *Concepts of Criticism* (New Haven and London: Yale University Press, 1963), pp. 69-127. Below, in Chapter 7, Sections II and IV, it will be seen that, in general, the Renaissance takes a more joyous and optimistic attitude toward worldly goods and pleasures than does the Baroque. This is in accord with the latter's increased emphasis on religion, for post-Tridentine Catholicism stresses the importance of heavenly, rather than earthly, treasures. Baroque pessimism concerns wordly existence only; it is optimistic with regard to the hereafter (see Chapter 2, Section XII below). Regarding literary style, the Baroque prefers complexity of form (euphuism, contortion, ambiguity and obscurity of metaphor, complicated structure, cultivation of the sensory, the witty, and the gestural), as opposed to the simplicity of the Renaissance; see Green, *Spain,* I, p. 209. Alemán's *Guzmán* is unanimously classified by critics as a Baroque work; see Green, *Spain and the Western Tradition,* IV (Madison, Milwaukee, and London: University of Wisconsin Press, 1966), p. 217.

6. Parts of this section are based on Enrique Moreno Báez, *Lección y sentido del "Guzmán de Alfarache"* (Madrid: C. S. I. C., 1948), pp. 22-45, although his interpretations of data are often quite different from those here set forth.

7. The following critics agree that *Guzmán* was read as a book of entertainment: Fonger de Haan, "Pícaros y ganapanes," in *Homenaje a Menéndez y Pelayo* (Madrid: V. Suárez, 1899), II, p. 170; Ludwig Pfandl, *Historia de la literatura nacional española en la Edad de Oro* (Barcelona: Sucesores de Juan Gili, 1933), p. 305; Francisco Ayala, *Experiencia e invención* (Madrid: Taurus, 1960), p. 156. That the seventeenth century Englishman was interested primarily in *Guzmán*'s adventures is seen in an adaptation of 1655-1656, which preserves only the plot. For the popularity of *The Rogue* in England at this time, see Dale B. J. Randall, *The Golden Tapestry* (Durham, N. C.: Duke University Press, 1963), pp. 182-84. Edwin B. Knowles has shown that *Don Quixote* was regarded only as a jestbook in seventeenth century England ("Cervantes and English Literature" in *Cervantes across the Centuries,* eds. Angel Flores and M. J. Benardete

[New York: Dryden, 1947], pp. 267-93). It is well known that Cervantes' Spanish contemporaries emphasized only the comic qualities of his novel; see, for example, Luis Astrana Marín, Introduction, ed. of *Don Quixote* (Madrid: Editorial Castilla, [1947?]), p. lii, and Agustín G. de Amezúa y Mayo, *Opúsculos histórico-literarios*, I, p. 256.

8. See Buenaventura Carlos Aribau, "Discurso sobre la primitiva novela española," in *Biblioteca de Autores Españoles*, III (Madrid: Rivadeneyra, 1846), p. xxv; and Agustín G. de Amezúa y Mayo, *Cervantes, creador de la novela corta española*, I (Madrid: C. S. I. C., 1956), p. 427.

9. "Bosquejo histórico sobre la novela española," in *Biblioteca de Autores Españoles*, XXXIII (Madrid: Rivadeneyra, 1854), p. lxxi.

10. "Nueva interpretación de la novela picaresca," *Revista de Filología Española*, XXIV (1937), pp. 343-62.

11. Prologue to ed. of *Guzmán*, in *La novela picaresca española* (Madrid: Aguilar, 1943), p. 159.

12. *Lección y sentido del "Guzmán de Alfarache,"* cited in note 6 above.

13. "De la intención y valor del *Guzmán de Alfarache*," *Romanische Forschungen*, LXXI (1959), pp. 267-311.

14. See Celina S. de Cortázar, "Notas para el estudio de la estructura del *Guzmán de Alfarache*," *Filología, VIII* (1962), pp. 79-95, on which parts of this section are based.

15. References are to Part and page of *The Rogue: or, The Life of Guzman de Alfarache*, trans. James Mabbe, 3rd ed. (London: Robert Allot, 1634). The pagination of this edition coincides with that of the first (London: Edward Blount, 1622-1623).

16. Joseph E. Gillet, *Propalladia and Other Works of Bartolomé de Torres Naharro*, III (Bryn Mawr, Pa. [Menasha, Wisconsin: George Banta Publishing Co.], 1951), p. 497.

17. Two sequels to *Lazarillo* did continue the anticlerical tendencies of the original, but significantly, both were published outside of Spain, in Antwerp and Paris. The first, of unknown authorship, appeared in 1555; the second, by Juan de Luna, was published in 1620.

18. See Amado Alonso, "Lo picaresco de la picaresca," *Verbum*, XXII (1929), pp. 321-38.

19. The italics in quotes are always Mabbe's.

20. For an identical concept of honor, see *Don Quixote*, I, 33. Throughout this study it will be seen that Cervantes often expresses ideas that coincide with Alemán's against the currents of the time.

21. In similar fashion, Juan Ruiz, the Archpriest of Hita, had invited his audience to change in his *Libro de buen amor* whatever it did not like; see the Clásicos Castellanos ed. (Madrid, 1954), II, p. 257.

22. See Agustín G. de Amezúa y Mayo, "Formación y elementos de

la 'novela cortesana'," in *Opúsculos histórico-literarios,* I, pp. 257-66. This situation is analogous to that which prevailed in Italy a century or two earlier. There too storytellers justified their licentious collections on the grounds that they taught "noble and useful lessons of moral philosophy"—part of the subtitle of Sebastiano Erizzo's *Le Sei Giornate* (*The Six Days* [1567]). Perhaps the best example is Giambattista Giraldi Cinthio, who represents the Catholic reaction of the Council of Trent to the earlier novelists. Giraldi intercalates long moralistic digressions in his tales, but at the same time pens some of the raciest stories to be found in any literature.

23. The following section is based in part on the excellent study of André Vasquez de Prada, "La moralité dans le roman picaresque," *La Table Ronde,* No. 191 (1963), pp. 65-81.

24. See Sobejano (cited in note 13 of this chapter), pp. 277-82.

25. The motif of the suitor who slanders his lady in order to win her is very old, dating back to the Greek novel of Chariton, *Chaereas and Callirhoe* (second century A.D.). Its numerous versions include episodes in Johanot Martorell's *Tirant lo Blanch* (*Tirante the White* [1490]), a Spanish book of chivalry, in Ariosto's *Orlando Furioso* (1516), and in Spensers' *Faerie Queene* (1590). The plot was given story form by Alciato, Bandello, Timoneda, and Belleforest. Della Porta and others dramatized the tale, and Shakespeare composed the most perfect version in his *Much Ado about Nothing.* (For bibliography and an excellent study of the slanderous suitor plot, see Geoffrey Bullough, *Narrative and Dramatic Sources of Shakespeare,* II [New York: Columbia University Press, 1958], pp. 62-139 and 532-34.)

Alemán undoubtedly knew the Spanish and Italian variants of the story, but did not follow any of them closely. His version is unusual because it combines the motif of the defamatory wooer with that of the woman who avenges her own honor, whereas in many treatments the lady is defended by a champion. The self-defense was necessary, once the favored suitor withdrew from the scene. A typically Baroque detail is that this rival retires to a religious life after his disenchantment with the lady.

26. See the article of Miguel Herrero cited in note 10 of this chapter.

27. J. A. van Praag, "Sobre el sentido del *Guzmán de Alfarache,*" in *Estudios dedicados a Menéndez Pidal,* V (Madrid: C. S. I. C., 1954), pp. 283-306, has attempted, without success, to show that Alemán was an adherent of Judaism and that all his references to Catholicism are to be interpreted ironically.

28. This is not to impugn the sincerity of Alemán's religious conviction. The point is that he makes an unnecessary display of his orthodoxy, perhaps with an interested motive.

29. Edmond Cros, "Deux épîtres inédites de Mateo Alemán," *Bulletin Hispanique,* LXVII (1965), pp. 334-36.

30. The question has been posed by Charles V. Aubrun, *Bulletin Hispanique,* LI (1949), p. 196.

31. In a short digression in I, ii, 9, Alemán observes that Spain's role in the world of international relations is on the wane. He is thus one of the first Golden Age writers to perceive the decadence into which his country was falling.

32. See Rodríguez Marín, *Discursos,* pp. 41-43.

33. By Otis H. Green, in his excellent chapter on "Optimism-Pessimism," in *Spain and the Western Tradition,* III (Madison and Milwaukee: University of Wisconsin Press, 1965), to which this section is indebted.

34. See Green, *Spain and the Western Tradition,* II (Madison and Milwaukee: University of Wisconsin Press, 1964), pp. 52-63. There is another example in *Guzmán,* II, iii, 7.

35. The device of the spider and the snake ultimately derives from Pliny's *Natural History,* X, 95, although Alemán may well have taken it from Pero Mexía's *Silva de varia leción* (*Forest or Collection of Historyes*), iii, 4; see Saura Falomir, ed. of *Guzmán,* I, note 367. On Alemán's other possible debts to Mexía, see Falomir, I, notes 297, 499, and II, 44, 116, 182, 241, 459, 604. Cervantes and other Golden Age writers made extensive use of Mexía's miscellany; see Carlos Clavería, "Humanistas creadores," in *Historia general de las literaturas hispánicas,* ed. Guillermo Díaz-Plaja, II (Barcelona: Editorial Barna, 1951), p. 454.

36. Green, *Spain,* III, p. 375.

Chapter Three

1. This chapter is indebted to Shermon Eoff's excellent study, "The Picaresque Psychology of Guzmán de Alfarache," *Hispanic Review,* XXI (1953), pp. 107-19, and to the brilliant analysis by A. A. Parker, "The Psychology of the 'Pícaro' in *El Buscón,*" *Modern Language Review,* XLII (1947), pp. 58-69.

2. See Yitzhak Baer, *A History of the Jews in Christian Spain* (Philadelphia: The Jewish Publication Society of America, 1961), II, pp. 310, 326, 438.

3. *A Catholic Commentary on Holy Scripture* (New York: Thomas Nelson & Sons, 1953), p. 1074. The passage is repeated, without promise of reward and in an unambiguous context, by Paul in Romans 12: 20.

4. *Ibid.*

5. Cervantes held the same opinion of honor and virtue; see Américo Castro, *El pensamiento de Cervantes* (Madrid: Editorial Hernando, 1925), pp. 362-68.

6. See Stephen Gilman, "Retratos de conversos en la *Comedia Jacinta* de Torres Naharro," *Nueva Revista de Filología Hispánica,* XVII (1963-1964), pp. 21, 27.

7. See Caro Baroja, *Los judíos,* II, pp. 335-43 (cited in Chapter 1, note 33).

8. Although it appears that Alemán himself practiced usury prior to 1599 (see Chapter 1, Section VII), it seems evident that in Part II of his novel he directs his criticism to those extortioners who were exploiting him about the time he was writing.

Chapter Four

1. After the present section was written, there came to my attention an article by Marcel Bataillon ("Les nouveaux chrétiens dans l'essor du roman picaresque," *Neophilologus,* XLVIII [1964], pp. 283-98) in which the eminent French Hispanist too assumes that Guzmán is a New Christian. Bataillon's conclusion about the rogue's ancestry is based solely on the possibility that his Levantine forebears were Jewish.

2. See Edward Glaser, "Two Anti-Semitic Word Plays in the *Guzmán de Alfarache,*" *Modern Language Notes,* LXIX (1954), pp. 343-48.

3. Stephen Gilman, "The Case of Alvaro de Montalbán," *Modern Language Notes,* LXXVIII (1963), pp. 121-22, points out that suspected recent converts were subjected to sharp scrutiny during the celebration of the Mass.

4. Miguel de Cervantes, *Obras completas* (Madrid: Aguilar, 1962), p. 293. On p. 294 the usual epithet of "effeminate" is applied to a Jew.

5. The question of the relationship between *Guzmán* and *El Buscón* needs further investigation. Fernando Lázaro Carreter, "Originalidad del *Buscón,*" in *Studia philologica: homenaje a Dámaso Alonso,* II (Madrid: Editorial Gredos, 1961), pp. 326-37, studies the problem, but does not mention what is probably the most important influence of Alemán on Quevedo: the New Christian background of the pícaros.

6. See E. H. Templin, "The Mother in the *Comedia* of Lope de Vega," *Hispanic Review,* III (1935), pp. 219-44. A mother is ridiculed in Lope de Rueda's *Eufemia* (Valencia, 1567), a play that reflects *Lazarillo*'s satire on honor.

7. See Ruth Pike, "The Image of the Genoese in Golden Age Literature," *Hispania,* XLVI (1963), pp. 705-14.

8. See Rodríguez Marín, *Documentos,* p. 16.

9. See Erik v. Kraemer, *Le Type du faux mendiant dans les littératures romanes depuis le Moyen Age jusqu'au XVII*[e] *siècle* (Helsingfors: Finska Vetenskaps-Societeten, 1944).

Chapter Five

1. Saura Falomir, ed. of *Guzmán,* II, note 192.

2. Another possibility is that Alemán had corresponded with Mey about publishing Part II of *Guzmán*—this would explain why Guzmán had written to Pompeyo but did not know him. Perhaps Alemán sent the completed part of his manuscript to Mey, and Martí intercepted it, as Sayavedra did with the rogue's luggage.

3. It may well be asked why Alemán, in his fictitious biography of his enemy, sends Martí to the Indies. The answer is to be found in the prejudices of the Golden Age: Spaniards looked down upon the New World because it embodied the materialistic desires of those who wanted to get rich quickly and also because it was the refuge of unsavory social types, among them, New Christians. See Américo Castro, Prologue to Javier Malagón's *Estudios de historia y derecho* (Jalapa: Universidad Veracruzana, 1966), pp. 15-20, and the bibliography there cited.

4. See the excellent article by Leon Livingstone, "Interior Duplication and the Problem of Form in the Modern Spanish Novel," *Publications of the Modern Language Association,* LXXIII (1958), pp. 393-406. Also valuable is Joseph E. Gillet's "The Autonomous Character in Spanish and European Literature," *Hispanic Review,* XXIV (1956), pp. 179-90.

5. See Castro, "Cervantes y Pirandello," in *Hacia Cervantes,* 2nd ed., pp. 377-85.

Chapter Six

1. This was pointed out by Robert H. Williams, "Satirical Rules of Etiquette in the *Siglo de Oro,*" *Hispania,* XIII (1930), pp. 293-300, on whom much of this section is based. The same conclusion was arrived at independently by Celina S. de Cortázar, "El *Galateo español* y su rastro en el *Arancel de necedades,*" *Hispanic Review,* XXX (1962), pp. 317-21.

2. See Courtney Bruerton, "*Las ferias de Madrid* de Lope de Vega," *Bulletin Hispanique,* LVII (1955), p. 58, for the date of the play. The scene is in Act II.

3. A comparison of portions of the two passages illustrates how well Alemán remembered Part I while penning his continuation:

Part I, ii, 8

"I stretcht forth my necke, bore out my brest, stood stiffe upon my legs, advancing one while this, and then that other foote; carrying my selfe in that vaine and idle fashion, that every one at last had found me out, and observing the strangenesse of my lookes, my Mimicke gestures, and often change of postures, they began to jest and scoffe at my folly. But as long as they lookt upon me, I ne're lookt into that; nor did I so much as once perceive, that my faults were the strings whereon their laughter plaid" (*Rogue,* I, 159).

Part II, iii, 2

"I stretcht out my legs and my brest, and lifting up my head and bearing up my neck somewhat stiffe, I made two or three short turnes . . . treading my steps in state . . . Whereat they laugh't a good; and I rested well contented. They made themselves merry and I was very well pleased" (II, 226).

4. See Américo Castro, ed. of plays by Tirso de Molina (Madrid: Clásicos Castellanos, 1922), p. 35, and Francisco Rodríguez Marín, ed. of *Don Quijote,* VII (Madrid: Atlas, 1948), p. 24, note 6. The principle that a lone man can not force a woman had wide acceptance in European literature and was illustrated by a well-known story: A woman accuses a man of rape, while he claims that she sold him her favors. A judge orders the seducer to pay a large sum to the erstwhile maiden. When she departs, the judge commands the accused to take the money away from her. He is unable to do so, which proves that the woman could have defended her alleged virginity had she so desired. The judge restores the money to its owner and rebukes the trollop. The tale is very old, occurring in the thirteenth century; see Jacques de Vitry, *The Exempla,* ed. Thomas Frederick Crane (London: Folk-Lore Society, 1890), story CCLV. Perhaps the most famous treatment is that of Cervantes in Part II, 45 of *Don Quixote,* where Sancho Panza is the judge. Barezzo Barezzi, the genial translator of *Guzmán de Alfarache* into Italian, remembered a version of this story and seeing its appropriateness at this point (II, iii, 2), inserted it into Alemán's novel. The tale is likewise found in the English translation, since Mabbe rendered Part II of *Guzmán* from the Italian version (see James Fitzmaurice-Kelly, Introduction to *The Rogue* [London: Constable, 1924], I, pp. xxxii-xxxvi).

5. See D. P. Rotunda, "The *Guzmán de Alfarache* and Italian *Novellistica,*" *Romanic Review,* XXIV (1933), p. 132, and Milton A. Buchanan, "Short Stories and Anecdotes in Spanish Plays," *Modern Language Review,* V (1910), p. 88.

6. On the Spanish attitude toward free will, see Green, *Spain,* II, Chapter VI.

7. See Thomas Hanrahan, S. J., *La mujer en la novela picaresca de Mateo Alemán* (Madrid: Ediciones José Porrúa Turanzas, 1964), pp. 63-72, on which most of this paragraph is based.

8. First published in Bartolomé José Gallardo, *Ensayo de una biblioteca española de libros raros y curiosos,* I (Madrid: Rivadeneyra, 1863), columns 1341-70. This influence is pointed out by Samuel Gili y Gaya, ed. of *Guzmán* (Madrid: Clásicos Castellanos, 1956), III, p. 183; V, pp. 71, 117-31.

9. See Karl Vossler, *Lope de Vega y su tiempo* (Madrid: Revista de Occidente, 1933), p. 15.

10. In similar fashion, at the end of *Don Quixote* the hero awakes from a deep slumber and declares that he is no longer the same man, due to God's mercy in showing him the error of his ways.

11. Although a Part III of *Guzmán* was written by Felix Machado de Silva toward the middle of the seventeenth century (first published in *Revue Hispanique,* LXIX [1927], pp. 1-340), it is far from being a picaresque novel. Guzmán is no longer a rogue, but a pious gentleman. In other words, Machado's protagonist descends from Alemán's repentant and disenchanted narrator, not from the adventurous pícaro. The action lasts only a few weeks and recounts a pilgrimage made by Guzmán.

Chapter Seven

1. For its use in the theater, see Milton A. Buchanan, "Short Stories and Anecdotes in Spanish Plays," *Modern Language Review,* IV (1908-1909), pp. 178-84, V (1910), pp. 78-89.

2. It will be recalled that this apt description is by Green, *Spain,* I, p. 207 (cited in Chapter 2, note 5 above).

3. See Francisco López Estrada and John Esten Keller, Introduction, *Antonio de Villegas' "El Abencerraje"* (Chapel Hill: University of North Carolina Press, 1964), pp. 13-15. (This title is somewhat misleading; López Estrada and Keller do not propose Villegas as the author of *The Abencerraje,* but simply announce that it is his version that they reproduce.)

4. Refences are to Sir Walter Lamb's translation, *Ethiopian Story* (London: J. M. Dent & Sons, 1961).

5. See Georges Cirot, "La maurophilie littéraire en Espagne au XVIe siècle," *Bulletin Hispanique,* XL (1938), pp. 157, 438; XLIV (1942), p. 101; XLVI (1944), p. 13; and Moreno Báez, *Lección y sentido,* pp. 181-85.

6. Another example of the mutual religious intolerance between

Christians and Moslems is Daraja's affirmation that ". . . they were in all things both of them so like, that nothing did difference them, but their Religion, whereof (out of the greatnesse of both their discretions) they never argued, that they might not dis-brother themselves" (*Rogue*, I, 75). After Pérez de Hita's *Guerras civiles,* the conversion of the Moorish protagonists became an obligatory part of the ending of Golden Age works.

7. There is also great interest in religion in the *Ethiopian History*: Theagenes and Chariclea are a priest and priestess, and there are numerous descriptions of sacrifices and religious practices.

8. Alemán had an ancient precedent for his moralizing in the *Ethiopian History,* where the author constantly extracts moral lessons from the novelistic situations.

9. Juan Bautista Avalle-Arce traces the Spanish diffusion of this tale in *Deslindes cervantinos* (Madrid: Edhigar, 1961), pp. 163-235.

10. See novels I, 42, 55; II, 4, 20, 56; III, 59.

11. See novels I, 14, 22, 51; II, 9, 22, 24.

12. Alemán was also influenced by the *Novela de las flores* (*Novel of the Flowers*), a verse imitation of Masuccio by the Licentiate Tamariz, a Sevillian writer of the second half of the sixteenth century. The following details, lacking in Masuccio, are found in both Tamariz and Alemán: 1) the setting in Spain; 2) Masuccio's captain of the watch becomes a city judge and is introduced before the seducer; 3) Masuccio's basket of herbs becomes a basket of flowers, containing jasmines, gillyflowers, and dog roses; 4) the slave says the abbess will buy gold thread weekly (not monthly); 5) the ladies conveying the heroine to the convent say they enter the house of a newlywed; 6) the fire in the seducer's house is caused by negligence; 7) the judge thinks that the heroine's spouse tolerates her infidelity; 8) the judge can not sleep because of his anger; 9) the slave plans the seduction and release of the victim; 10) the slave takes leftover food to the prison; 11) the jailer receives money from the slave. For a comparison of Tamariz' story with Masuccio's, see my forthcoming article, "Sources and Significance of the *Novelas del Licenciado Tamariz,*" to appear in *Romanic Review.*

13. W. G. Waters translation, *The Novellino* (London: Lawrence and Bullen, 1895), II, p. 148.

14. Following the narration of Dorotea's heroic defense of her virtue, Alemán says that she had a pleasant supper with her violator and went to bed with him. This willingness contradicts the picture Alemán has just painted of his heroine's chastity; the slip in characterization is due to poor assimilation of the source material taken from Masuccio.

15. See William L. Fichter, *Lope de Vega's "El castigo del discreto"*

together with a Study of Conjugal Honor in his Theater (New York: Instituto de las Españas en los Estados Unidos, 1925), p. 44, note 62.

16. For an excellent study of the conceits of courtly love, see Green, *Spain*, I, Chapter III.

Selected Bibliography

Works of Mateo Alemán

Translations of two odes by Horace: *Rectius vives* and *Eheu fugaces.* Originally published without indication of place, printer, or date; probably Madrid, 1598. Reproduced by R. Foulché-Delbosc, *Revue Hispanique,* XLII (1918), 482-85.

Prologue to *Proverbios morales* (*Moral Proverbs*) by Alonso de Barros, Madrid: Luis Sánchez, 1598. Reproduced by R. Foulché-Delbosc, *Revue Hispanique,* XLII (1918), 486-87.

Guzmán de Alfarache. Part I, Madrid: Várez de Castro, 1599. Part II, Lisbon: Pedro Crasbeeck, 1604. The standard edition is that of Samuel Gili y Gaya, Madrid: Clásicos Castellanos, 5 vols., 1926-1936. Valuable introduction and notes. Another good edition is by Joaquín Saura Falomir, Madrid: Ediciones Castilla, 2 vols., 1953. Excellent introduction and many notes supplementary to those of Gili. The only complete English translation is by James Mabbe: *The Rogue: or, The Life of Guzman de Alfarache,* London: Edward Blount, 1622-1623. Modern reprint, London: Constable, 4 vols., 1924 (The Tudor Translations). Mabbe's rendition is occasionally inaccurate and adds elements to the original.

San Antonio de Padua (*St. Anthony of Padua*). Sevilla: Clemente Hidalgo, 1604. No modern reprint.

Ortografía castellana (*Castilian Orthography*). México: Ieronimo Balli, 1609. Excellent modern reprinting with introduction by Tomás Navarro, México: El Colegio de México, 1950.

Prologue to Luis de Belmonte Bermúdez' *Vida del Padre Maestro Ignacio de Loyola* (*Life of Father Ignatius of Loyola*). México: Geronimo Balli, 1609. Available in Francisco A. de Icaza, *Sucesos reales que parecen imaginados de Gutierre de Cetina, Juan de la Cueva y Mateo Alemán,* Madrid: Fortanet, 1919, pp. 253-63.

Sucesos de D. Frai García Gera (Happenings of Fray García Guerra). México: Viuda de Pedro Balli, 1613. Carefully reproduced with introduction and extensive notes by Alice H. Bushee, *Revue Hispanique,* XXV (1911), 359-457.

Secondary Sources

Biography

Alvarez, Guzmán. *Mateo Alemán.* Buenos Aires: Espasa Calpe, 1953. Readable, based principally on Rodríguez Marín's monographs. Contains occasional factual errors.

Rodríguez Marín, Francisco. *Discursos leídos ante la Real Academia Española* . . . 2nd ed., Sevilla: Francisco de P. Díaz, 1907. The fundamental biography, carefully documented and with perspicacious interpretations of data.

——. *Documentos referentes a Mateo Alemán y a sus deudos más cercanos (1546-1607).* Madrid: Archivos, 1933. Reproduces or abstracts most of the known Alemán documents.

Bibliography

Foulché-Delbosc, R. "Bibliographie de Mateo Alemán. 1598-1615," *Revue Hispanique,* XLII (1918), 481-556. Thorough descriptions of most editions of Alemán's works. The author's exceptional erudition and painstaking method make this a model bibliography.

Ricapito, Joseph Virgil. "Toward a Definition of the Picaresque. A Study of the Evolution of the Genre Together with a Critical and Annotated Bibliography of *La vida de Lazarillo de Tormes, Vida de Guzmán de Alfarache,* and *Vida del Buscón.*" Unpublished doctoral dissertation (University of California, Los Angeles, 1966). A nearly exhaustive list of studies, with an excellent summary of each.

Simón-Díaz, José. *Bibliografía de la literatura hispánica,* V, Madrid: C. S. I. C., 1958, pp. 126-58. The most complete list of editions of Alemán's works; also enumerates many studies.

General Studies on the Spanish Picaresque Novel

Chandler, Frank Wadleigh. *Romances of Roguery.* New York: The Macmillan Company, 1899. Although much of this manual's positivistic criticism has become outmoded, it contains much useful information. Chandler's principal error is the assumption that "The society, then, which the picaro traverses is the main thing . . ." (p. 60). Little or no attention is paid to the psychology of the individual rogues.

Gili Gaya, Samuel. "La novela picaresca en el siglo XVI" and "Apogeo y desintegración de la novela picaresca," in *Historia general de las literaturas hispánicas,* ed. Guillermo Díaz-Plaja, III. Barcelona: Editorial Barna, 1953, pp. 81-103, III-XXV. The best brief introduction to the genre.

Selected Bibliography

Monte, Alberto del. *Itinerario del romanzo picaresco spagnolo.* Florence: Sansoni, 1957. The best comprehensive survey. Particularly good for bibliographical references.

Studies of "Guzmán de Alfarache"

Eoff, Sherman. "The Picaresque Psychology of Guzmán de Alfarache," *Hispanic Review,* XXI (1953), 107-19. An excellent analysis of Guzmán's personality and motivations.

Moreno Báez, Enrique. *Lección y sentido del "Guzmán de Alfarache."* Madrid: C. S. I. C., 1948. The only book-length study of *Guzmán.* Carefully written and documented, and therefore helpful for examining certain aspects of the novel. Its thesis—that the purpose of *Guzmán* is to illustrate the Tridentine doctrine of original sin, free will, and grace—is unacceptable. See the penetrating review by Charles V. Aubrun, *Bulletin Hispanique,* LI (1949), 194-98.

Sobejano, Gonzalo. "De la intención y valor del *Guzmán de Alfarache,*" *Romanische Forschungen,* LXXI (1959), 267-311. The best comprehensive study of Alemán's novel. Convincingly refutes the religious thesis of Moreno Báez, pointing out that *Guzmán* is an educational work that shows the dangers confronting a child bereft of moral instruction. Compares *Guzmán* with *Lazarillo de Tormes,* studies the apocryphal Part II and its effect on Alemán's continuation, and examines the present-day relevance of *Guzmán.*

Index

This index includes references to authors and historical personages mentioned in the text, the notes, and the bibliography. References to works may be found under the authors' names. Titles of anonymous works are also listed.

Abencerraje, El, 147, 148, 149, 151-57
Aesop, 135
Alarcón, Juan Ruiz de, 24, 37, 40
Albertinus, Aegidius, 48
Alcalá Yáñez, Jerónimo de, 40, 47
Alciato, Andrea, 175
Alemán, Alonso (uncle of Mateo), 13, 17
Alemán, Alonso (cousin of Mateo), 17, 35, 37, 38
Alemán, Ana Urbana, 7, 24, 36
Alemán, Antonio, 8, 24, 36
Alemán, Beatriz, 13
Alemán, Catalina, 36
Alemán, García Jerónimo, 13, 14
Alemán, Hernando, 7, 13, 14, 15, 17
Alemán, Jerónima, 13
Alemán, Juan, 13
Alemán, Juan Agustín, 14, 36
Alemán, Leonor (aunt of Mateo), 13
Alemán, Leonor (sister of Mateo), 14
Alemán, Margarita, 8, 24, 25, 36, 39
Alemán, *Poca Sangre,* 14
Alemán, Violante, 14
Alonso, Amado, 174
Alter, Robert, 172
Alvarez, Guzmán, 184
Amezúa y Mayo, Agustín G. de, 170, 174
Anthony of Padua, St., 8, 19, 27, 31, 32, 33, 34, 35, 36, 183
Aribau, Buenaventura Carlos, 174
Ariosto, Lodovico, 175
Aristotle, 68
Astrana Marín, Luis, 171, 174
Aubrun, Charles V., 176, 185
Avalle-Arce, Juan Bautista, 181
Avellaneda, Alonso Fernández de (*pseud.*), 129, 172
Averoni, Atanasio de, 34
Awdeley, John, 44
Ayala, Francisco, 173

Baer, Yitzhak, 176
Baeza, Pedro de, 27, 30
Bandello, Matteo, 68, 121, 158, 160, 175
Barezzi, Barezzo, 179
Barros, Alonso de, 8, 21, 169, 183
Bataillon, Marcel, 172, 177
Baudelaire, Charles Pierre, 78
Belleforest, François de, 175
Bellow, Saul, 50
Belmonte Bermúdez, Luis de, 8, 38, 183
Bentivoglio, Alessandro, 121
Bible, 70, 94, 176
Bleiberg, Germán, 169
Boccaccio, Giovanni, 68, 108, 117, 128, 157, 160, 161, 162, 163
Bruerton, Courtney, 178
Buchanan, Milton A., 179, 180
Bullough, Geoffrey, 175
Bushee, Alice H., 171, 183

Calderón, Francisca, 8, 24, 25, 32, 33, 35, 36
Calderón, María, 25, 35, 36
Calderón de la Barca, Pedro, 24
Caro Baroja, Julio, 171, 177
Cary, Joyce, 50
Casa, Giovanni della, 131
Castiglione, Baldesar, 131
Castillo Solórzano, Alonso del, 47
Castro, Américo, 172, 177, 178, 179
Castro y Bellvis, Guillén de, 105
Cela, Camilo José, 50
Cervantes Saavedra, Miguel de, 21, 22, 23, 24, 25, 37, 40, 41-43, 54, 71, 72, 76, 86, 99, 102, 110, 124, 129, 136, 138, 144, 145, 146, 147, 157, 167, 171, 172, 173, 174, 176, 177, 179, 180
Chandler, Frank Wadleigh, 184
Chariton, 175
Charles I, 14
Chaves, Cristóbal de, 139
Cicero, Marcus Tullius, 23
Cirot, Georges, 180
Clavería, Carlos, 176
Correa Calderón, E., 170
Cortázar, Celina S. de, 174, 178
Cortés de Tolosa, Juan, 46
Cronan, Urban, 172
Cros, Edmond, 176

Dávila, Fray Diego, 22, 66, 67
Defoe, Daniel, 49
Delicado, Francisco, 44, 124
Della Porta, Giovanni Battista, 175
Demar, Francisco, 27
Demosthenes, 23
Domenichi, Lodovico, 103, 106, 134
Doni, Anton Francesco, 134
Dostoevski, Fëdor Mikhailovich, 78

Enero, Agustina de, 40
Enero, Juana de, 13, 14, 40
Eoff, Sherman, 176, 185
Erizzo, Sebastiano, 175
Espinel, Vicente, 47
Espinosa, Catalina de, 7, 8, 16, 17, 19, 24, 27, 36, 79, 133, 134
Espinosa, María de, 170
Eulenspiegel, Till, 45

Falcón, Jaime Juan, 116
Ferdinand the Catholic, 148, 149, 154, 155
Fichter, William L., 181
Fielding, Henry, 49, 75
Fitzmaurice-Kelly, James, 179
Fletcher, John, 147
Flores, Juan de, 128
Foulché-Delbosc, R., 170, 171, 183, 184
Freudenhold, Martinus (*pseud.*), 48
Fugger (family), 20

García, Carlos, 44
García, Domingo, 36
García Guerra, Fray, 8, 37, 38, 171, 183
Gestoso y Pérez, José, 170
Gili y Gaya, Samuel, 180, 183, 184
Gillet, Joseph E., 172, 174, 178
Gilman, Stephen, 177
Giovanni Fiorentino, Ser, 117
Giraldi Cinthio, Giambattista, 134, 175
Glaser, Edward, 177
González, Estebanillo, 48
Gracián, Baltasar, 23, 170
Gracián Dantisco, Lucas, 131
Gray, Malcolm Jerome, 169
Green, Otis H., 172, 173, 176, 180, 182
Grillo, Esteban, 109
Grimmelshausen, Hans Jacob Christoffel von, 48
Groussac, Paul, 172
Guicciardini, Francesco, 134
Guillén, Claudio, 169, 172

Haan, Fonger de, 173
Hanrahan, Thomas, 180

Hardy, Thomas, 75
Heliodorus, 146, 149-57
Henríquez, Ureña, Pedro, 171
Heraclitus, 83
Hernández de Ayala, Alonso, 16
Herrero, Miguel, 55, 172, 174, 175
Homer, 44, 152
Horace, 21, 38, 68, 183
Icaza, Francisco A. de, 183
Isabella the Catholic, 148, 149, 154, 155

Juan Manuel, Don, 68

Keller, John Esten, 180
Knowles, Edwin B., 173
Kraemer, Erik v., 178

Lancelot of the Lake, 157
Lazarillo de Tormes, 44, 46, 47, 48, 50, 53, 60-66, 70, 73, 75, 80, 84, 86, 88, 96, 97, 98, 101, 104, 105, 109, 110, 111, 137, 140, 172, 174, 177, 184, 185
Lázaro Carreter, Fernando, 172, 177
Ledesma, Pedro de, 36
León, Beatriz de, 13
León, Fray Luis de, 40, 84
Leonard, Irving A., 170, 171
Lesage, Alain René, 49, 54, 75
Libro de Alexandre, 124
Libro de Apolonio, 124
Livingstone, Leon, 178
Lizardi, José Joaquín Fernández de, 50
López, Diego, 24, 27, 29, 30, 121
López, Francisco, 28, 29, 30, 31, 121, 122
López, Miguel, 24, 27, 29, 30, 121
López de Enero, Juan, 14
López de Ubeda, Francisco, 47
López Estrada, Francisco, 180
López Pinciano, Alonso, 72, 152
Loyola, St. Ignatius of, 8, 38, 183
Luján, Micaela de, 32
Luján de Sayavedra, Mateo (*pseud.*; also see Martí, Juan), 26, 113, 119, 122, 123
Luna, Alvaro de, 161, 162
Luna, Juan de, 46, 174

Mabbe, James, 101, 130, 174, 179, 183
Machado de Silva, Felix, 180
Mal Lara, Juan de, 15, 170
Mann, Thomas, 50
Manrique, Jorge, 141
Martí, Juan, 26, 30, 33, 47, 48, 69, 74, 75, 78, 81, 82, 113-29, 139, 142, 143, 144, 147, 171, 172, 178, 185
Martínez, Miguel, 28, 29, 30, 121
Martorell, Johanot, 175
Massinger, Philip, 147
Masuccio Salernitano, 138, 146, 160-66, 181
Maticorena Estrada, Miguel, 169
Mayans y Siscar, Gregorio, 54
McGrady, Donald, 171, 181
Medici, Ferdinand I de', 86
Medina, Jose Toribio, 171
Mexía, Pero, 176
Mey, Pedro Patricio, 119, 178
Miguel, Francisco, 120
Monte, Alberto del, 185
Montemayor, Jorge de, 159
Moratín, Leandro Fernández de, 54
Moreno Báez, Enrique, 55, 69, 173, 180, 185
Muriel, Josefina, 170, 171

Narváez, Rodrigo de, 153, 154
Navarrete, Eustaquio Fernández de, 55
Navarro, Tomás, 183

Parker, Alexander A., 176
Pérez de Hita, Ginés, 148, 152, 153, 156, 181
Pérez de Montalbán, Juan, 133

Pérez Pastor, Cristóbal, 170
Pfandl, Ludwig, 170, 173
Philip II, 18, 19, 21, 22, 46, 80
Philip III, 22, 28
Pike, Ruth, 177
Pirandello, Luigi, 124
Pliny, 176
Porter, Thomas, 147
Praag, J. A. van, 175

Quevedo y Villegas, Francisco de, 24, 47, 53, 75, 102, 103, 104, 131, 135, 139, 140, 172, 177, 184

Randall, Dale B. J., 173
Ranier of Anjou, 161, 162
Rauhut, Franz, 172
Ricapito, Joseph Virgil, 184
Rodríguez de Montalvo, Garci, 124, 152
Rodríguez Marín, Francisco, 169, 170, 171, 172, 176, 178, 179, 184
Rojas, Fernando de, 44, 157, 158, 165
Romero, José Rubén, 50
Rosso, Juan Bautista del, 8, 25, 27, 29, 30, 31, 33, 34, 35, 40, 41, 171
Rosso, Lorenzo del, 41
Rotunda, D. P., 179
Rueda, Lope de, 177
Ruiz, Juan, 99, 173, 174

Salas Barbadillo, Alonso Jerónimo de, 47
San Pedro, Diego de, 124, 157, 158, 159
Santa Cruz, Melchor de, 134, 135
Saura Falomir, Joaquín, 169, 176, 178, 183
Schons, Dorothy, 171
Sforza, Ippolita, 121
Shakespeare, William, 175
Simón-Díaz, José, 170, 171, 184
Smollett, Tobias, 49
Sobejano, Gonzalo, 55, 56, 175, 185
Spenser, Edmund, 175
Stendhal (pseud. of Marie Henri Beyle), 50
Straparola, Gian Francesco, 108

Tamariz, Licentiate, 181
Templin, E. H., 177
Thackeray, William, 50
Timoneda, Juan, 106, 107, 138, 175
Tirso de Molina (pseud. of Gabriel Téllez), 40, 94, 99, 105, 133
Tolstoi, Lyev Nikolayevich, 75
Torres Villarroel, Diego de, 49
Tristan and Iseult, 157
Twain, Mark (Clemens, Samuel), 50

Valbuena Prat, Angel, 55
Valdés, Luis de, 22, 31, 170
Vasquez de Prada, André, 175
Vega Carpio, Lope de, 24, 32, 40, 68, 105, 132, 133, 134, 135, 140
Vélez de Guevara, Luis, 47, 133
Virgil, 152
Vitry, Jacques de, 179
Volante, Gregoria, 24, 36
Vossler, Karl, 180

Wellek, René, 173
Williams, Robert H., 178

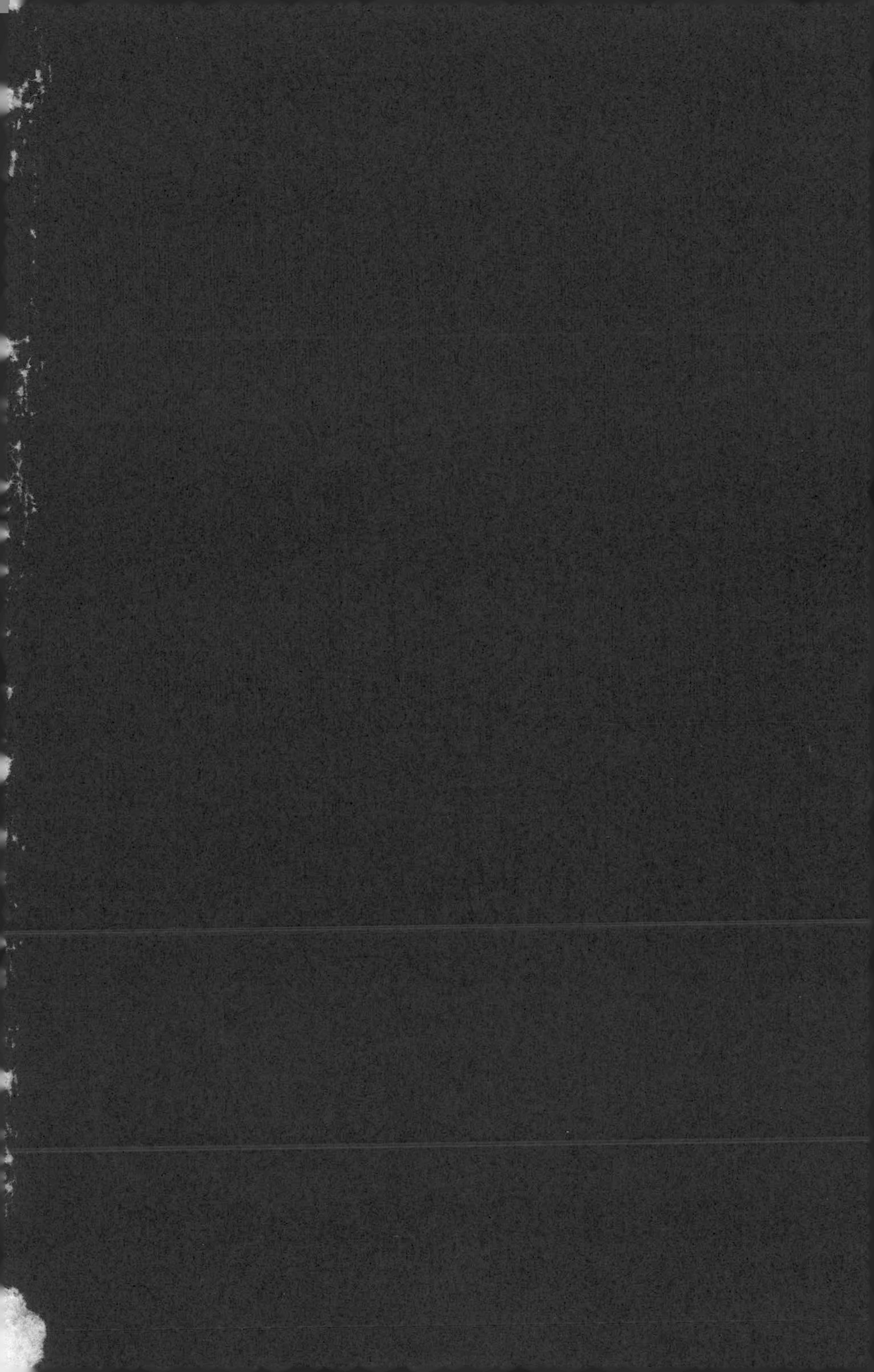